Our Catholic Devotions

Our Catholic Devotions

A Popular Guidebook

Therese Johnson Borchard

A Crossroad Book
The Crossroad Publishing Company
New York

The Crossroad Publishing Company
370 Lexington Avenue, New York, NY 10017

Scripture quotations are from the New Revised Standard
Version Bible, © 1989 by the Division of Christian Education
of the National Council of the Churches of Christ
in the United States of America. Used by permission.

Sections of chapters one and two have been previously
published in *The Truth About the Rosary* and *What You
Should Know About the Stations of the Cross*, Liguori
Publications, and are reprinted with permission.

Acknowledgments are found on pp. 143-144,
which constitute an extension of the copyright page.

Printed in the United States of America

Library of Congress Cataloging-in-Publication Data

Borchard, Therese Johnson.
　　Our Catholic devotions : a popular guidebook / Therese Johnson Borchard.
　　　　p.　　cm.
　　Includes bibliographical references.
　　ISBN 0-8245-1739-3 (pbk.)
　　1. Catholic Church—customs and practices.　　I. Title.
BX2110.B67　　1998　　　　　　　　　　　　　　　　　97-43776
248.3'088'22—dc21　　　　　　　　　　　　　　　　　CIP

2 3 4 5 6 7 8 9 10 03 02 01 00 99

*For my mother,
who taught me
the beauty and power
of our Catholic devotions*

CONTENTS

WHAT ARE DEVOTIONS?

One story immediately comes to mind when I think about the rich assortment of devotions that belong to our Catholic tradition.

My mother and father had just separated, and my mother was saying a novena to Saint Thérèse of Lisieux. Tradition holds that during the nine days of this novena, Saint Thérèse will shower upon the pray-er "roses from heaven," as is referred to in the novena prayer:

> Saint Thérèse, the Little Flower, please pick me a rose from the heavenly garden and send it to me with a message of love. Ask God to grant me the favor I thee implore (*name intention*), and tell him I will love him each day more and more.

It was the ninth day of my mom's novena, when Mr. Miller, our next-door neighbor who kept an impeccable garden, decided to prune his rose bushes. He began trimming off all of the roses fully in bloom in order to preserve the fresh, tender buds. As he lay the several dozens of flowers beside the bushes, my sister came along and asked if she could take them. She was merely trying to earn good points with Mom since she had been in trouble that week.

Upon Mr. Miller's permission, my sister began to make several trips back and forth from his garden to our kitchen, and searched out every possible vase to hold the bouquets. With the skill of an artist, she placed each rose in its proper place, until every corner of the kitchen was spilling over with beautiful flowers.

After a long day, my mom walked into the room that looked and smelled like a heavenly rose garden, and, tears forming in her eyes, she remembered it was her last day of the novena to Saint Thérèse of the Rose.

OUR LOVE OF DEVOTIONS

My story is just one of many that illustrates the special love Catholics have for devotions. Our tradition is full of stories like mine, that describe the symbolic meaning and power of our devotions. These stories tell of a conversion point, when something that is a part of our daily lives, some-thing tangible, brings alive for us the profound truth of our faith.

Devotions help many of us to experience God more personally. They can often make clear in our lives the grace of God to which we are sometimes blinded. And they may point us to the sacred—to faith, hope, and love—in an affective medium that other expressions of our faith cannot. Devotions, as a form of popular piety, inspire us to live our lives within the Christian context, and to adhere more closely to the stories of the Gospel.

OUR FEAR OF DEVOTIONS

Our special love for devotions comes with a certain cautiousness, a fear of what devotions can become when done as isolated practices of piety outside the proper Christian and Catholic context. And, because the Church before the Second Vatican Council had an exaggerated emphasis on them, devotions are, for many of us, reminders of the "old Church"; they may bring to mind the rigidity and other negative elements of the pre-Vatican II Church that are best left behind. We are careful in practicing devotions because we see their dangerous potential to create and support a type of simplistic faith that involves superstition.

However, in our vigilance, most of us are intrigued and awed by these very special Catholic expressions. It only takes one pilgrimage to Lourdes or Mexico City to appreciate their power and continuing influence in today's faith culture. The endless crutches hanging over the holy water at Lourdes and the original image of Our Lady of Guadalupe, framed on the center wall of that city's crowded basilica, are signs that Catholic devotions are alive and well in our day.

DEFINITION OF DEVOTIONS

But what, exactly, is a devotion? What makes Lourdes worthy of an expensive flight across the Atlantic, while we doubt the visions of Our Lady reported by many persons closer to home? What, for example, constitutes a novena? Could I pray to my deceased father for nine consecutive days and declare with confidence that I've made one?

The *New Catholic Encyclopedia* defines religious devotions as:

> practices of piety that give concrete expression to
> the will to serve and worship God by directing it
> to some particular object, such as a divine
> mystery, person, attribute, or even to some
> created reality as that is related to God.

The HarperCollins Encyclopedia of Catholicism
(referred to hereafter as the *Encyclopedia of
Catholicism*) explains devotions as "nonliturgical
prayer forms that promote affective attitudes of
faith."

Finally, Michael Walsh describes devotions in
the *Dictionary of Catholic Devotions* as the
"religious purpose or object to which dedicated
attention is given . . . distinguished from the
Church's liturgical forms of worship."

I understand Catholic devotions as being a
combination of these three: as an organized form
of prayer, separate but related to the liturgy, that
deepens my personal relationship with God,
strengthens my commitment to the Christian
community, and leads me to a deeper
understanding of the Paschal Mystery, the reality
to which my faith continually looks.

QUALITIES OF TRUE DEVOTIONS

The Church is very vigilant with regard to
popular devotions. In an effort to prevent supersti-
tious behavior and simplistic attitudes in devotional practice, the authorities of the Church have
outlined three criteria in determining if a practice
is a true devotion. Following are the three qualities
of true devotions:

1) True devotions are grounded in sound
   doctrinal content and based on solid
   theology.
2) True devotions have sensible and
   imaginative appeal.
3) True devotions guide persons to a deeper
   spiritual life.

The Church reaffirmed its strong support of
popular devotions at the Second Vatican Council,
as is recorded in the *Constitution on the Sacred
Liturgy*:

> Popular devotions of the Christian people,
> provided they conform to the laws and norms of
> the Church, are to be highly recommended,
> especially where they are ordered by the
> Apostolic See. (*Constitution on the Sacred
> Liturgy*, no. 13)

However, this document goes on to explain the
proper context in which devotions must be done,
and the overriding purpose of them:

> But such devotions should be drawn up that they
> harmonize with the liturgical seasons, accord
> with the sacred liturgy, are in some way derived
> from it, and lead the people to it . . . (*Constitution
> on the Sacred Liturgy*, no. 13)

Devotions are empty expressions if they fail to embody in some way the Christian story—the death and resurrection of Jesus Christ—and the ongoing presence of the Holy Spirit in our lives. However, when they point to the story of Christian redemption—God incarnate in our world—and illumine the hope and truth of the cross, they are invaluable instruments in leading souls more directly to God.

HISTORY OF DEVOTIONS

Devotions were born to fill a spiritual need of the faithful. They have, in part, served those persons throughout history who weren't comfortable with, or did not understand, the complexities of the liturgy. However, it can be said that all believers benefit from devotions, because these popular practices add an affective, imaginative, or sensible element to worship that isn't always a part of liturgical prayer. A pattern threaded throughout history, participation in popular devotions increases when liturgical prayer and ritual are not accessible enough.

Although the cultivation of popular devotions as a distinct prayer form is, relatively speaking, somewhat modern (post Reformation), traces of the more traditional devotions are found in

scripture and appear in the earliest records of
Christianity. For example, the first traces of the
legend of Our Lady's pilgrimage in Jerusalem—
eventually becoming the devotion we know today
as the Stations of the Cross—appeared in a Syriac
text assigned to the fifth century.

DEVOTIONS TODAY

To this day popular devotions fill a spiritual
need of the faithful. They offer us an affective,
tangible expression of faith; they present us with a
personable medium to communicate with God;
and they make possible a sensible experience of
the sacred in our everyday lives.

Popular devotions aid a person in preparing
for, understanding, and participating more fully in
the celebration of the Eucharist and all kinds of
liturgical worship. When done in the proper
context and for the right purpose, they foster and
promote worship of God, inspiring the faithful to
cooperate and take part in the Christian story.

In his book *The Stations of the Cross: An
Account of Their History and Devotional Purpose*,
the Jesuit Herbert Thurston teaches us how to
understand and appreciate devotional piety. His
words, for me, best capture the inherent beauty
and power of our Catholic devotions:

> Once the symbolic character of so many of our
> aids to devotion is understood and allowed for,
> we can use them without danger as stepping
> stones to a higher knowledge and deeper love of
> the Source of all grace. We venerate them for
> what they symbolize and for that which they help
> to bring nearer to us.

With this end in mind, I present in this book twelve of the most popular devotions: the Rosary, Stations of the Cross, Marian devotion, the scapular, the Miraculous Medal, Liturgy of the Hours, eucharistic adoration, devotion to the Saints, devotion to the Sacred Heart, novenas, pilgrimages, and icons and sacred art.

Each chapter includes a brief history of the devotion, its theological significance, practical information on saying or doing the devotion, and contemporary reflections.

CHAPTER ONE

THE ROSARY

HAIL, HOLY QUEEN

Hail, holy Queen, mother of Mercy.
Hail, our life, our sweetness
and our hope.
To thee do we cry,
poor banished children of Eve;
to thee do we send up our sighs,
mourning and weeping,
in this vale of tears.
Turn then, most gracious advocate,
thine eyes of mercy toward us;
and after this our exile, show us unto
the blessed fruit of thy womb, Jesus.
O clement, O loving,
O sweet virgin Mary.

HISTORY OF THE ROSARY

Naturally we are tempted to think that the Rosary has always been in the form that it is today; that it came to us as a neat package from Mary herself, the beads and prayers all properly formatted. Not the case. Like most of our devotions, its development into the form that we have today was evolutionary.

MARY AND THE ROSE GARDEN

The word "rosary" comes from the Latin *rosarium*, which means "rose garden." The affiliation of the rose garden with Mary dates back to the Hebrew Scriptures, in the Song of Songs, where the author writes about a beautiful woman abiding in a garden. She is described as "a rose of Sharon, a lily of the valleys" (Song of Songs 2:1).

For Christians this passage and the entire Song of Songs symbolize the nuptial love between Christ and his people. Thus, the woman is understood to be the Virgin Mary and the garden of immortality is recognized as the rose garden of Our Lady.

The association of roses and rose gardens with Mary took on greater significance in Catholic tradition in the twelfth century with the writings of Bernard of Clairvaux and his Cistercian order. Religious art also promoted the rose as a symbol for Mary.

Paintings of Mary in rose gardens became popular themes in art, especially during the fifteenth century. And the beads, though not always present in the paintings, were implicitly part of the scene since they, and the prayers said with them, were already called rosaries by this time.

USE OF BEADS IN PRAYER

There is no one date of origin for the Rosary. Assigning this devotion an approximate beginning point depends heavily on how you define it. If we understand the Rosary as a strand of beads used to count prayers, its origins extend way back before the birth of Christ, to the ninth century B.C., when the Hindus began to use prayer beads.

Most likely the first Christians to come up with a method like beads for counting prayers were the earliest of the Desert Fathers, those who fled to the desert in the third century to pray incessantly in order to achieve spiritual purity.

This group of hermits, who had memorized the psalms, would decide on a number of psalms and/or prayers to be said each day. Some would use pebbles to count their prayers, either dropping one to the ground or shifting one to a second pile for each psalm recited.

As years went on, the method of counting became more sophisticated. By the eleventh century, it was common for the religious and devout laity to carry with them strings of beads or knotted cords called "paternosters."

DEVELOPMENT OF THE PRAYERS

The prayers that are included in the Rosary developed in tandem with the use of paternosters. As devotion to Jesus and Mary increased in the eleventh and twelfth centuries, vernacular prayers, especially the Our Father (*Pater Noster*) and the Hail Mary (*Ave*), were recited by the laity as a substitute for the Latin psalms.

Similar to the Psalter—a liturgical book containing the psalms and biblical canticles that was used by religious—prayers were collected and organized into groups of 50 for use by laity in popular piety.

Eventually, phrases referring to the lives of Jesus and Mary—which evolved into the mysteries—were interjected between the prayers, creating an appropriate framework or context for them.

MYSTERIES OF THE ROSARY

It wasn't until several centuries later, after most of the prayers had developed and people were using the beads with these prayers, that the mysteries appeared in a form recognizable to our own. Dominic of Prussia, a Carthusian monk living in the early fifteenth century, wrote a set of fifty meditations—statements of Christian belief called *clausulae*—one for each of the fifty Aves. Eventually the clausulae and Aves were grouped into decades, each decade beginning with an Our Father.

CHURCH APPROVAL

The Church's approval of the Rosary, or at least its official recognition, was conferred in 1571, much to the credit of the Dominicans and the formation of the Rosary Confraternity. The Confraternity published volumes on the Rosary that contributed to its popularization. Popes Pius V and Leo XIII were instrumental, as well, in the promotion of the Rosary.

THE MYSTERIES OF THE ROSARY

The Joyful Mysteries

—The Annunciation
—The Visitation
—The Nativity
—The Presentation
—The Finding of Jesus in the Temple

The Sorrowful Mysteries

—The Agony in the Garden
—The Scourging of Jesus
—The Crowning with Thorns
—The Carrying of the Cross
—The Crucifixion

The Glorious Mysteries

—The Resurrection
—The Ascension
—The Descent of the Holy Spirit
—The Assumption
—The Coronation of Our Lady

THEOLOGY OF THE ROSARY

The theology of the Rosary is found in the mysteries: the unifying cord with which the beads are threaded and the meaningful backdrop against which the prayers are posed. Without such a structure—the story of Christ's incarnation, death, and resurrection—the Rosary would not be the profound devotion that it is. Said outside of the context of the Christian story, the decades of the Rosary make little sense; the prayers become mere repetitions of words.

The mysteries organize the reflections interjected between Our Fathers and Hail Marys into a continuous meditation on the life of Jesus and Mary; the fifteen mysteries are also a summary of the liturgical year. In meditating on the mysteries, we are reflecting on our human condition: our freedom from limitation through Christ's birth; our own suffering and imminent death through Christ's agony and crucifixion; and our hope for new life in Christ's resurrection and ascension.

PRAYERS OF KARL RAHNER

The prayers of Karl Rahner best articulate how to meditate on the mysteries of the Rosary. In the

following reflections, he prays the Joyful, Sorrowful, and Glorious Mysteries.

Prayer at Christmas

God, the Eternal Mystery of our Life, by the
birth of Your own word of love in our flesh You
have made the glory of Your life in its eternal youth
into our life, and have caused it to appear in
triumph. Grant us that when we experience the
disappointments of our lives we may be enabled to
believe that Your love, which You Yourself are and
which You have bestowed upon us, is the eternal
youth that is our own true life.

Reflection on the Passion

Lord Jesus Christ, our Savior and Redeemer, I
kneel before Your blessed cross. I want to open my
spirit and my heart to contemplate Your holy
sufferings. I want to place Your cross before my
poor soul that I might know it a little better, that I
might receive more deeply into my heart all that
You did and suffered, and that I might realize who it
was for whom You suffered. May your grace be
with me, the grace to shake off the coldness and
indifference of my heart, to forget my everyday life
for at least this half-hour, and to dwell with You in
love, sorrow, and gratitude.

The Ascension and Presence of the Lord

Lord, when You return even as You have departed from us, as a true man, then may You find Yourself in us as the one who bears all, is patient, is faithful, is kind, is selfless; as the one who cleaves to the Father even in the darkness of death, the one who loves, the one who is joyful. Lord may You find Yourself in us, being what we would so much wish to be yet are not.

But Your grace has not only endured. In reality, it has come to us simply in virtue of the fact that You, having ascended and been enthroned at the right hand of God, have poured out Your Spirit into our hearts. And so we truly believe that against all experience You do continue Your life in us even though it seems to be only ourselves—Ah! almost always only ourselves and not You—that we find within ourselves.

You have ascended into heaven and are seated at the right hand of God with our life. You are coming back with that life in order to find Your life in ours. And the fact that You will find it there—that will be our eternity even when we, together with all that we are and have lived and have possessed and have borne, shall have entered into the glory of Your Father through Your second coming.

EDWARD SCHILLEBEECKX
THE PRAYER OF THE ROSARY

■ The value of the prayer of the Rosary is to be found in its concentration on the saving mystery of the Redemption. It was Christ who brought this redemption, but Mary is actively present in and associated with the whole of this historical order of salvation. The Rosary is a synthetic Christological creed, a *symbolum* or compendium of dogma and doctrine, in the form of a prayer of meditation, a summary, in prayer, of the whole of the dogma of the Redemption.

■ The Rosary enables us to follow Mary's development, the growth of her life. In faith and hope we are able to experience all the phases of the mystery of Christ, to proceed from the joys of the mother and her Child, to go beyond the sufferings endured by the Redeemer and his mother and eventually to reach the point where we share in Mary's happiness in her Son's victory and triumph. Christ—personal redemption, Redemption itself—is at the centre of this Marian prayer.

■ When we pray the Rosary we are focusing our attention inwardly on the living mysteries of Christ. Outwardly, we do no more than murmur, almost breathlessly, the Hail Marys, while our gaze is directed upwards, in faith, to each mystery in turn. What we are in fact saying to Mary, throughout this inward prayer, is no more than "Thank you."

■ The prayer of the Rosary can teach us how to model our *fiat* on Mary's "typical" example, and how to express this personal assent to all the various stages of our own lives—in joy, in suffering and in triumph.

■ When we pray the Rosary, we are doing what Mary herself did . . . It was by prayerful reflection that she learned how to understand the mystery of Christ and to become fully aware of her own particular place in the economy of the Redemption. It is only by becoming more and more familiar with the "mystery of Christ" which *embraces* the mystery of Mary, that we too shall come to an understanding of our place and our concrete vocation in the redeemed world.

—*Mary, Mother of the Redemption*

THE ROSARY TODAY

Today the Rosary consists of the recitation of fifteen decades of Hail Marys, each decade beginning with an Our Father and followed by a Glory Be to the Father (the Doxology). Each decade is also accompanied by a meditation that usually names the mystery and includes a short reflection on it.

BEGINNING THE ROSARY

The Rosary can begin and end in various ways. Most commonly, we start with the Apostles' Creed, recited as we hold the crucifix that is part of the Rosary pendant. We move on to say the Our Father and three Hail Marys, represented by the four beads next to the crucifix. We complete the pendant part of the Rosary with a Glory Be to the Father.

THE DECADES

We proceed into the body of the Rosary by announcing the first joyful mystery, the Annunciation, and reading a short reflection on it. Then we begin the prayers of the first decade with an Our

Father followed by ten Hail Marys, each represented by a bead. We conclude the decade with a Glory Be to the Father, and sometimes the O My Jesus prayer introduced in the apparition of Our Lady of Fatima: "O my Jesus forgive us our sins. Save us from the fires of Hell. Lead all souls to Heaven, especially those in most need of your mercy."

After a moment of silence, the second joyful mystery is announced, its meditation read, and the process is repeated until the last glorious mystery is announced or meditated upon, and its decade of prayers said.

There are fifteen mysteries in all, and so fifteen decades. After finishing a set of mysteries, we return to the first bead of the Rosary (excluding the pendant beads) to start another set. However, we often pray only five decades, or one set of mysteries.

ENDING THE ROSARY

Most commonly the Rosary is terminated with the recitation of the Hail Holy Queen and the prayer from the Feast of the Rosary. The Memorare and the Litany of the Blessed Virgin Mary are occasionally recited at the end as well.

PRAYERS OF THE ROSARY

The Hail Mary

Hail Mary, full of grace, the Lord is with thee; blessed art thou among women and blessed is the fruit of thy womb, Jesus. Holy Mary, Mother of God, pray for us sinners, now and at the hour of our death. Amen.

The Our Father

Our Father, Who art in heaven, hallowed be Thy name, Thy kingdom come; Thy will be done on earth as it is in heaven. Give us this day our daily bread; and forgive us our trespasses, as we forgive those who trespass against us. And lead us not into temptation; but deliver us from evil. Amen.

The Glory Be

Glory be to the Father, and to the Son, and to the Holy Spirit. As it was in the beginning, is now, and ever shall be, world without end. Amen.

CHAPTER TWO

STATIONS OF THE CROSS

Let us behold
what care and pains our loving Lord
hath taken of our salvation;
Let us learn to travaille courageously
and like devout and holy pilgrims
to follow His steps,
who hath left us an example
of His blessed life and passion.

—*Jan Pascha*, The Spiritual Pilgrimage

HISTORY OF THE STATIONS

Yesterday's Christians were no different from
today's in that they yearned to walk the same steps
as Jesus, and to witness the holiest of places:
where Jesus died, was buried, and rose again.
Thus, the Stations of the Cross began as pilgrimages to the Holy Land.

THE FIRST PILGRIMS

The Way of Sorrows, or the road to Calvary, is
said to have been first traversed by Mary, but it is
not until the fourth century that we have sufficient
records of people venerating important places
associated with Jesus' life, death, and resurrection.

Among the first documented pilgrimages to
the Holy Land are those of a Bordeaux pilgrim, in
333 A.D., and the Lady Egeria in 380 A.D. Their
narratives describe the veneration of certain places
in Jerusalem, especially Mount Calvary, where
Jesus died, and the tomb where Jesus was buried.
In the early years of the fourth century, the Roman
Emperor Constantine erected shrines at these and
other holy places. The most important shrine—the
Church of the Holy Sepulchre—was built at the
burial place of Jesus.

IMITATIVE SHRINES

As the desire to walk the Way of Calvary increased in the succeeding centuries, so too did the need to replicate the experience—an alternative pilgrimage, so to speak, for those who couldn't make the arduous journey. Thus, imitations of the more important shrines in Jerusalem sprang up in various places. The earliest set of imitative shrines outside of Palestine was erected in the fifth century at the Monastery of San Stefano in Bologna.

Imitations became more common as the devotion was promoted by veterans of the Crusades who had visited the Holy Land. By the fourteenth century, copies of the Church of the Holy Sepulchre and other shrines—"Little Jerusalems" as they were sometimes called—could be found all over Europe.

THE SEVEN FALLS

By the late fifteenth century, the Stations of the Cross reached another stage in its development: an arrangement of carvings in stone or wood popularly known as the "Seven Falls" (in each of the carvings Jesus was understood to be sinking or falling under his burden). Like the larger imita-

tions, the carvings and pictorial representations of
the holy places in Jerusalem were intended to
recall the events of the Passion story.

ARRANGEMENT OF THE STATIONS

The Stations of the Cross did not always
consist of fourteen stations. As late as the
seventeenth century, sites irrelevant to Jesus' death
and resurrection were mixed in with those
venerated as part of the Passion.

The narratives of early travelers suggest that
stations were added a few at a time. The last
four—Jesus being nailed to the cross, Jesus' death,
Jesus being removed from the cross, and Jesus
being placed in the tomb—come directly from
Scripture. The meeting with Mary, Simon helping
Jesus, and the weeping women of Jerusalem pop
up in the late thirteenth-century and early
fourteenth-century narratives. Veronica and the
offering of her veil appears later in the fifteenth
century. It is unclear as to when the first two falls,
the sentence of Pilate, and the stripping of the
garments were added.

The number fourteen first appeared in manuals
of devotion published during the sixteenth century.
The number and sequence of the stations, however, was set by Pope Clement XII in 1731.

ROLE OF THE FRANCISCANS

When the Franciscans took over custody of the shrines in the Holy Land in 1342, they saw it as part of their mission to promote devotion to these places and to the Passion of Christ by way of the Stations of the Cross. Members of the Franciscan order were known in Jerusalem and throughout Europe as the official statesmen, authorities, and chief promoters of the Stations. These religious were largely responsible for developing artistic representations and carvings of the holy scenes and arranging them in churches throughout the West. Leonard of Port Maurice was especially known for his efforts in popularizing the Stations. He is said to have erected more than five hundred sets of stations in the span of twenty years—between 1731 and 1751—the best known among them located in the Coliseum at Rome. Popes Clement XII and Benedict XIV also helped define and propagate the Stations.

THE FOURTEEN STATIONS

—*The First Station:*
Jesus is condemned to death on the cross

—*The Second Station:*
Jesus accepts his cross

—*The Third Station:*
Jesus falls the first time

—*The Fourth Station:*
Jesus meets his sorrowful Mother

—*The Fifth Station:*
Simon of Cyrene helps Jesus carry
his cross

—*The Sixth Station:*
Veronica wipes the face of Jesus

—*The Seventh Station:*
Jesus falls the second time

—*The Eighth Station:*
Jesus meets and speaks to the women
of Jerusalem

—*The Ninth Station:*
Jesus falls the third time

—*The Tenth Station*
Jesus is stripped of his garments

—*The Eleventh Station*
Jesus is nailed to the cross

—*The Twelfth Station:*
Jesus dies on the cross

—*The Thirteenth Station:*
Jesus is taken down from the cross

—*The Fourteenth Station:*
Jesus is placed in the tomb

THEOLOGY OF THE STATIONS

The purpose of the devotion of the Stations of the Cross is to enrich our life of prayer and faith, and to turn us to Christ Crucified. The Way of the Cross is an invitation to gaze on the sufferings of the man from Nazareth, our Lord and Redeemer. As aids to sorrowful contemplation, the fourteen scenes or halting places help us to remember and honor the Passion of our Lord.

THE SEVEN LAST WORDS

I again refer to the prayers of Karl Rahner to best demonstrate the profound theology and devotional benefit of the Stations. In the following pages I have taken small excerpts from seven of his prayers, each based on the last words of Jesus before his death. In *Prayers for a Lifetime*, Rahner explains the importance of these words that tell the story of Christ's Passion.

> I want to meditate upon Your seven last words upon the cross . . . Let them penetrate into my heart. . . . That I might understand them. That I might never again forget them. . . . Those words will be either an eternal beginning, or an everlasting end, for me.

KARL RAHNER
THE SEVEN LAST WORDS

*Father, forgive them; for they do not
know what they do.* Luke 23:34

You are hanging upon the cross. You nailed
Yourself to it. . . . Those who prepared all this for
You stand there beneath the cross. . . . They stand
around. They laugh. . . . But you said: "Father,
forgive them, for they know not what they do."
. . . Where in all Your tortured and tormented soul
did You find a place for words like these?

*Amen, I say to you, this day you will be
with me in Paradise.* Luke 23:43

You are now in the agony of death, Your heart
is filled to the brim with anguish, and yet You still
have a place in that heart for the sufferings of
another.

*Woman, behold your son; Son, behold your
Mother.* John 19:26

Even here in Your agony Your love is quick to
express the tenderness which in this world every
son feels for his mother. And through Your death
even the tender, precious things of our world such
as this are consecrated and sanctified, these things
which make the heart gentle and the earth beautiful.

*My God, my God, Why have You
forsaken Me?* Matthew 27:46

In this night of the senses and of the spirit, in
this desert that consumes everything in Your heart,
Your soul is still in prayer. The dreadful wasteland
of a heart devastated by suffering becomes in You a
solitary call to God.

I thirst. John 19:28

You thirsted for me. You thirsted after my love
and my salvation: as the deer thirsts for the spring,
so does my soul thirst for you.

It is finished. John 19:30

This end is Your fulfillment. For whoever
comes to the end in love and fidelity has reached
fulfillment. Your failure is Your triumph.

*Father, into Your hands I commend
My spirit.* Luke 23:46

You let Yourself be taken from Yourself. You
give Yourself over with confidence into those
gentle, invisible hands. We who are weak in faith
and fearful for our own selves experience those
hands as the sudden, grasping, merciless, stifling
grip of blind fate and of death. But You know that
they are the hands of the Father.

THE STATIONS TODAY

The devotion of the Stations of the Cross is practiced today by meditating on fourteen chosen representations of the sufferings of Christ on his way to Calvary. At each station—which, in the strictest sense, consists of a wooden cross blessed by an authorized priest—a person halts, allowing time for sorrowful contemplation. The devotion is still done in imitation of those who travel to the Holy Land to honor the places of Jesus' walk to crucifixion.

INDULGENCES

Although indulgences (remissions before God of the temporal punishment due to sins) are an old-fashioned concept, they deserve mention in the discussion of the Stations because they contributed much to the growth and popularity of the Stations.

Today a person can still gain a plenary indulgence (versus a partial indulgence) if the following conditions are met:

1) The person must make the Stations with a contrite heart.
2) The person must be in the state of grace.

3) The person must meditate on the Passion of Christ.

4) The person must proceed from one station to the next, without interruption.

As part of the Way of the Cross, persons will sometimes recite one Our Father, Hail Mary, and Glory Be to the Father, and/or other prayers at each station; however, this is not necessary to gain the indulgence. The form of prayer that is most commonly said with the Stations is taken from the writings of St. Alphonsus Liguori.

THE FIFTEENTH STATION

Although most people include fourteen stations as part of the devotion—ending with Christ's burial—there has been much discussion among modern liturgists about adding Christ's resurrection as a final station. Some argue that the devotion is incomplete without reference to the Resurrection, while others maintain that, since the place where Jesus was buried is also where he rose from the dead, the fourteenth station theologically includes the Resurrection.

POPE JOHN PAUL II
THE SCRIPTURAL STATIONS

On Good Friday, 1991, Pope John Paul II led a crowd of people at the Roman Colosseum through the Stations of the Cross. He made the Stations in a manner different from the usual way, using stations based entirely on Gospel texts. Some of the traditional ones were kept, while others were dropped and new ones were added.

—The First Station:
   The Agony of Jesus in the Garden of Olives

—The Second Station:
   The Betrayal and Arrest of Jesus

—The Third Station:
   The Sanhedrin Condemns Jesus

—The Fourth Station:
   Peter Denies Jesus

—The Fifth Station:
   Pilate Condemns Jesus to the Cross

—The Sixth Station:
   Jesus Is Scourged and Crowned With Thorns

—The Seventh Station:
Jesus Is Mocked by the Soldiers and Given His Cross

—The Eighth Station:
Simon the Cyrenian Helps Jesus Carry His Cross

—The Ninth Station:
Jesus Meets the Women of Jerusalem

—The Tenth Station:
Jesus Is Crucified

—The Eleventh Station:
Jesus Promises Paradise to the Penitent Criminal

—The Twelfth Station:
Jesus Speaks to His Mother and to His Disciple

—The Thirteenth Station:
Jesus Dies on the Cross

—The Fourteenth Station:
The Burial of Jesus

—The Fifteenth Station:
Jesus Rises From the Dead

CHAPTER THREE

MARIAN DEVOTION

Having entered deeply into the history of salvation, Mary . . . unites in her person and re-echoes the most important doctrines of the faith: and when she is the subject of preaching and worship she prompts the faithful to come to her Son, to his sacrifice and to the love of the Father.

—*Vatican II*, Lumen Gentium

HISTORY OF MARIAN DEVOTION

The first evidence of devotion to Mary is found in the Gospels. Luke especially presents Mary as a holy woman of faith and founding member of the earliest Christian community.

FIRST MARIAN BLESSINGS

In Luke's Gospel, Elizabeth, Mary's cousin, greets the Mother of the Lord with one of the first Marian blessings, which eventually became the first part of the Hail Mary we recite today.

> Blessed are you among women, and blessed is
> the fruit of your womb! And why has this
> happened to me, that the mother of my Lord
> comes to me? For as soon as I heard the sound of
> your greeting, the child in my womb leaped for
> joy. And blessed is she who believed that there
> would be a fulfillment of what was spoken to her
> by the Lord. (Luke 1:42-45)

Mary, in turn, recites a canticle, the Magnificat, in which she praises the Lord for her place in the history of salvation.

> My soul magnifies the Lord,
>   and my spirit rejoices in God my Savior,

> for he has looked with favor on the lowliness of
> > his servant.
> > Surely, from now on all generations will call
> > me blessed. (Luke 1:46-48)

PATRISTIC THEOLOGY

Various images of Mary emerged from the biblical depictions of Mary—found primarily in the Gospels, the Acts of the Apostles, and the Book of Revelation—in the centuries following the birth of Christ. In the writings of the Church Fathers, three themes were especially prevalent: Mary as the new Eve; Mary as ever-Virgin; and Mary as Mother of God. This last theme, Mary as *Theotokos* or "God-bearer," was disputed by Nestorius, patriarch of Constantinople, in the early fifth century, but he was overruled by the Council of Ephesus in 431; the Council's statement that Mary was the Mother of God strengthened Marian devotion in the following centuries.

MEDIEVAL PIETY

During the next period, from the eighth to the fifteenth century, there was greater concentration on Mary's role as intercessor or mediatrix of God's grace. As heavenly queen, she was seen as having maternal influence over God, able to pacify

Christ's anger and obtain mercy for sinners.
During this time, Mary's power to save became
the focus of attention.

THE REFORMATION

As devotion to Mary spread in the fifteenth
century with rapid diffusion of Marian literature,
Protestant Reformers became increasingly uncomfortable with devotion to her because of the
Church's position regarding Mary's intercessory
power. However, the Council of Trent (1545-63)
defended Marian devotion, further encouraging
invocation to her. Catholic tradition further
separated from the Protestant faiths with regard to
Mary when two Marian doctrines were declared
dogmas by papal decrees: the Immaculate Conception (1854) and the Assumption (1950).

VATICAN II

With these two Marian dogmas and the
reported apparitions throughout Europe in the
nineteenth and twentieth centuries, Marian
devotion became somewhat isolated from
Scripture and the liturgy. Thus, it was one of the
goals of the Second Vatican Council to re-situate
Marian devotion within the mainstream truths of
the Catholic faith.

THEOLOGY OF MARIAN DEVOTION

Devotion to Mary is an important expression of Christian life because Mary has been assigned an irreplaceable function within the Christian order of salvation.

MARY'S ROLE IN REDEMPTION

Because of her maternal quality, Mary manifests one aspect of Christ's redemption which could not be made explicit by Christ himself; insofar as she makes Christ's redemption in some way more lucid, she adds to it. Mary plays a paramount role in the redemptive mystery of Christ, and thus to the fundamental mystery of our Christian faith. As Edward Schillebeeckx explains in *Mary, Mother of the Redemption*:

> A task of great importance for all men was assigned by God to Mary in connection with the vocation of mankind given to us in the person of Christ. Her unique place within the plan of salvation is an appeal made by God to all men. We are bound, in faith and love, to recognize this call and to give our assent to it, because we must, in our constantly growing consciousness of faith, enter into the scheme of salvation in accordance with God's objective will.

MARIAN DEVOTION IN PROPER CONTEXT

Because Mary explicates God's maternal redeeming love, she is an important character in the story of our redemption; however, she does not add anything new to God, as God is all-powerful and all-knowing. Thus, it is important to keep Marian devotion in its proper context: integrated into the theologies of Christ and the Church.

Elizabeth A. Johnson describes the proper place of Marian devotion in her article "Blessed Virgin Mary" in the *Encyclopedia of Catholicism*:

> Honoring Mary should occur within the bounds of a rightly ordered faith and thus not over-shadow the one triune God: Father, Son, and Spirit. It should keep clearly in view that Christ alone is the merciful Savior and one Mediator between God and human beings. It should give due recognition to the working of the Holy Spirit in the gift of grace. And it should give expression to the newly recognized connection between Mary and the Church.

MARY AS EXEMPLAR

The *Dogmatic Constitution on the Church* (*Lumen Gentium*) of the Second Vatican Council situates Mary in the midst of the communion of saints, those deceased persons who exemplify for us the truths of our faith. Mary, in her eternal "Amen" to Christ, is an excellent model of faith and symbol of obedience. As the Mother of God, she stands above the rest of the saints, teaching us how to live in the unconditional love of her Son.

Mary, however, is much more than an example of faith and love. She comforts the pilgrim Church on earth, offering the people of God hope and grace through Christ. Elizabeth Johnson, again, describes Mary's solidarity with the faithful:

> The central theological image is that of Mary as a woman of faith, preeminent among the disciples, the first of the redeemed in Christ. While not significant on the world stage, her simple human life shows forth the victory of God's grace. Her historical role as the mother of Jesus, while unique, is interpreted through the lens of graced existence, which she shares in solidarity with all the people of God. Only in this way can she be a model, or symbolic embodiment, of the Church.

MARIAN DEVOTION
ACCORDING TO VATICAN II

Mary has by grace been exalted above all angels and men to a place second only to her Son, as the most holy mother of God who was involved in the mysteries of Christ: she is rightly honored by a special cult in the Church. . . . The various forms of piety towards the Mother of God, which the Church has approved within the limits of sound and orthodox doctrine, according to the dispositions and understanding of the faithful, ensure that while the mother is honored, the Son . . . is rightly known, loved and glorified and his commandments are observed.

The sacred synod teaches this Catholic doctrine advisedly and at the same time admonishes all the sons of the Church that the cult, especially the liturgical cult, of the Blessed Virgin, be generously fostered, and that the practices and exercises of devotion towards her, recommended by the teaching authority of the Church in the course of centuries be highly esteemed, and that those decrees, which were given in the early days regarding the cult images of Christ, the Blessed Virgin and the saints, be religiously observed. But it strongly urges theologians and preachers of the word of God to be careful to refrain as much from all false exaggeration as from too summary an attitude in considering the special dignity of the Mother of God. Following the study of Sacred Scripture, the Fathers, the doctors and liturgy of the Church, and under the guidance of the Church's magisterium, let them rightly illustrate the duties and privileges of the Blessed Virgin which always refer to Christ, the source of all truth, sanctity, and devotion. Let them carefully refrain from whatever might by word or deed lead the separated brethren or any others whatsoever into error about the true doctrine of the Church.

Let the faithful remember moreover that true devotion consists neither in sterile nor transitory affection, nor in a certain vain credulity, but proceeds from true faith, by which we are led to recognize the excellence of the Mother of God, and we are moved to a filial love towards our mother and to the imitation of her virtues.

—*Lumen Gentium*, no. 66-67

MARIAN DEVOTION TODAY

There are several kinds of Marian devotion that exist in contemporary popular piety. There are practices, such as the wearing of a special scapular or the Miraculous Medal, which are covered in the next two chapters. There are liturgical celebrations, such as the Solemnity of the Immaculate Conception (December 8), and the Solemnity of Mary Mother of God (January 1). There is devotion to the Immaculate Heart of Mary. And there is devotion to Our Lady as she appeared in various apparitions, described briefly here.

APPARITIONS OF OUR LADY

Of the ways to honor Mary listed above, devotion to Mary as she has appeared throughout history in well-documented visions is the most popular form of devotion today. It is likely that at least one person you know has traveled to the site of a Marian apparition—in devotion to the Blessed Virgin, or in curiosity. The most popular places of pilgrimage include Lourdes, Mexico City (Guadalupe), Medjugorje, and Fatima.

There have been countless reports of Marian apparitions throughout time, but only a few have

NOTABLE MARIAN APPARITIONS
WITH ECCLESIASTICAL APPROVAL

—*Guadalupe, Mexico*
Mary appeared four times in 1531 to
Juan Diego

—*Paris, France (Rue de Bac)*
Mary appeared three times in 1830 to
Catherine Labouré

—*La Salette, France*
Mary appeared in 1846 to Melanie
Matthieu and Maximin Giraud

—*Lourdes, France*
Mary appeared 18 times in 1858 to
Bernadette Soubirous

—*Pontmain, France*
Mary appeared in 1871 to a group of
peasant children

—*Fatima, Portugal*
Mary appeared six times in 1917 to Lucia
dos Santos, and Francisco and Jacinta Marto

—*Beauraing, Belgium*
Mary appeared 33 times from 1932-33 to
five children

—*Banneux, Belgium*
Mary appeared eight times in 1933 to
Mariette Beco

received ecclesiastical approval. Reported visions
are studied very carefully; they are submitted to an
evaluation process in which they have to meet
certain criteria. One of the requirements is that
authentic texts of the revelation must be procured,
without corrections and amendments; a second is
that the visionary should show spiritual progress
after the apparitions.

In all of the apparitions, the Blessed Virgin has
a similar message: she confirms our sinfulness, but
reassures us of Christ's redemption; she urges us
to repent and pray continuously; and she speaks of
peace.

CHAPTER FOUR

THE MIRACULOUS MEDAL

MEMORARE

Remember, O most gracious Virgin Mary, that never was it known that anyone who fled to thy protection, implored thy help, or sought thy intercession, was left unaided. Inspired with this confidence, I fly unto thee, O Virgin of virgins, my Mother. To thee do I come, before thee I stand, sinful and sorrowful. O Mother of the Word Incarnate, despise not my petitions, but in thy clemency, hear and answer me. Amen.

HISTORY OF THE MIRACULOUS MEDAL

Although the devotion of the Miraculous Medal
is relatively new—beginning with the apparition
of the Blessed Virgin to Catherine Labouré in
1830—the wearing of religious medals is found
far back in the early Christian ages.

HISTORY OF RELIGIOUS MEDALS

In the fourth century, Saint Zeno, Bishop of
Verona in northern Italy, cited the wearing of
medals as an example of the Church's practice of
sanctifying pagan customs. He also described the
use of medals to commemorate the baptism of new
Christians. From about the fourth century until the
eighth century, it is thought that pieces of money,
coins of the late empire, were converted to religious medals for pious use.

Religious medals as they are known today
began to appear in the sixteenth century. In 1566,
Pope Pius V blessed and indulgenced a medal
bearing the image of Jesus and Mary. The wearing
and blessing of medals spread rapidly thereafter,
so that by the seventeenth century every city in
Europe had its own medals featuring Jesus, Mary,
or a favorite saint or devotion.

APPARITION TO CATHERINE LABOURÉ

The Miraculous Medal is one of the most popular religious medals worn today by the faithful. The origin of this specific medal dates back to the apparition of Mary to Catherine Labouré in November of 1830.

As Saint Catherine—a daughter of Charity of St. Vincent de Paul—knelt in prayer at the motherhouse in Paris, the Virgin stood before her on a globe, crushing a serpent beneath her foot. From her outstretched hands streamed forth rays of light, symbolizing graces. An oval frame gradually enclosed the Virgin, and around its border appeared the words, "O Mary, conceived without sin, pray for us who have recourse to thee."

Everything then reversed, and Catherine saw a large letter "M" surmounted by a bar and a cross, beneath which appeared the Immaculate Hearts of Mary and Jesus—one crowned with thorns, the other pierced with a sword.

After both sides of the medal were shown in detail to the saint, she heard a voice saying, "Have a medal struck after this model. All who wear it will receive great graces. They should wear it around the neck."

PAPAL APPROVAL

The first medals were struck in June of 1832, with the permission of Archbishop de Quélen of Paris. In the years that followed, so many miracles were attributed to the medal that it became known as the Miraculous Medal, and millions were being made. Papal approval was quickly won, following the sudden and unexpected conversion of Alphonse Ratisbonne, a Jew hostile to Catholicism, as he visited a church in Rome in January of 1842.

FEAST OF THE MIRACULOUS MEDAL

On July 23, 1894, Pope Leo XIII published a rescript instituting a feast, with a Mass and Office, in honor of the Immaculate Virgin Mary of the Miraculous Medal to be celebrated annually—proper to the Vincentian Fathers and Daughters of Charity—on November 27. In this papal document, he writes:

> It was fitting that Mary's motherly affection, which was made manifest with such efficacy and generosity by means of the Miraculous Medal, should be ever remembered, and at the same time that the veneration of the faithful for the Immaculate Conception should be given increased fervor.

THEOLOGY OF THE MIRACULOUS MEDAL

A wealth of Marian theology is found in the imagery and symbolism of the Miraculous Medal. As H. P. Delany, C.M., author of *The Miraculous Medal*, explains:

> [The Miraculous Medal] unfolds a most absorbing mystery, a vital and far-reaching truth. It shows us how Jesus Christ, our one and only Redeemer, the Sovereign "Mediator between God and men" (I Timothy 2:5), has willed to associate Mary, a human creature, intimately and inseparably with Himself in the meritorious acquisition of the Grace of Redemption and in the application of that precious grace to the souls of all men, in the sanctification and salvation of souls, to the end of time.

FACE OF THE MEDAL

On the face of the Miraculous Medal is the figure of Mary crushing a serpent as rays of lights stream forth from her outstretched hands and are diffused over the globe upon which she is standing. This entire image—set in the framework of her own prayer: "O Mary, conceived without sin, pray for us who have recourse to thee"—provides the faithful with symbols of basic Marian themes

in theology, such as Mary as the Immaculate
Conception, Mary as the Mediatrix of All Graces,
and Mary the Virgin Most Powerful.

BACK OF THE MEDAL

The reverse of the medal contains important
Marian symbols, as well. The letter "M" is surmounted by a cross; underneath it are two hearts,
one crowned with thorns and the other pierced
with a sword. These objects are encircled by
twelve stars. The complete image symbolizes the
reason and source of Mary's unique and vital role
in the divine economy of grace.

SYMBOLISM OF THE MEDAL
H. P. DELANY, C.M.

The Miraculous Medal is remarkably rich in symbolism. It presents us—or rather, by graciously giving us her Medal of the Immaculate Conception, our Immaculate Mother presents us—with a beautiful little Cameo of Mariology. All the signs engraved on the Medal, be it remembered, were revealed by her, in all their detail, to Saint Catherine Labouré, and are, therefore, her own ingenious handiwork.

They are brimful of meaning. They portray and proclaim high and holy things, great and profound mysteries. They represent Mary's sublime prerogatives, her special privileges and powers, as well as the reason and source of these prerogatives, in the divine economy of grace. They also depict the personal and living relations between the Mother and the Son, between our spiritual Mother and each of us, in the Eternal Father's merciful and loving plan of Redemption and Salvation.

Interwoven, the one with the other, these signs symbolize the intimate and inseparable association of Mary with Jesus in the vital work, first of all, of our reconciliation with our Heavenly Father, and, then, of our supernatural life of grace on earth and of our life of glory . . . in Heaven.

—*The Miraculous Medal*

THE MIRACULOUS MEDAL TODAY

Although the Miraculous Medal is still one of the most popular religious medals worn today, it is not nearly as popular as it was in the days before the Second Vatican Council.

THE MEDAL AS A SACRAMENTAL

In the *Constitution on the Sacred Liturgy*, Vatican II redefined sacramentals, such as the Miraculous Medal and all medals, encouraging a new understanding of their intrinsic relationship to the sacraments, and, therefore, their ability to sanctify human life. This document defines sacramentals as:

> Sacred signs which bear a resemblance to the sacraments. They signify effects, particularly of a spiritual nature, which are obtained through the Church's intercession. By them men are disposed to receive the chief effects of the sacraments, and various occasions in life are rendered holy.
> (*Constitution on the Sacred Liturgy*, no. 60)

In eliminating any tendencies toward superstition in the use of religious medals that may have been part of pre-Vatican II devotion, contemporary

Catholic teaching strongly asserts that religious medals should not be used or regarded as magic charms or amulets. The *New Catholic Encyclopedia* states:

> Catholic teaching attributes no intrinsic power to medals, blessed or not. The medal is a symbol that recalls to the believer his faith and his religious duties. Such a reminder moves him to acts of reverence to God or to Christ, immediately or mediately through the sacred person or event represented by the medal. It is not from the medal that the believer expects help or on which he puts reliance. The medal occasions acts of faith and hope in God whom it represents either directly or indirectly.

THE BLESSING OF MEDALS

Indulgences are attached to the Miraculous Medal with the proper blessing. To be properly blessed the medals must:

1) Be blessed with a prayer directed to obtaining some favor from God, through the intercession of Christ and of the person who may be represented on the medal.
2) Represent a person or event that has been approved and certified by the Church.

3) Be made of some solid substance.
4) Be blessed by a priest who has been granted the necessary faculties to bless it.

Following is part of a special rite for blessing of the Miraculous Medal found in the Roman Ritual:

O Almighty and Merciful God, Who through the manifold apparitions on earth of the Immaculate Virgin Mary deign ever to perform wonders for the salvation of souls: graciously bestow your blessing on this medal; so that they who cherish and devoutly wear it may both enjoy her protection and obtain your mercy. Through Christ Our Lord.

As the priest bestows the holy medal on the recipient, he says:

Receive this holy medal, wear it faithfully, and give to it the veneration it deserves: so that the most loving and Immaculate Lady of Heaven may protect and defend you; and renewing the prodigies of her love, may mercifully obtain for you whatever you suppliantly ask from God, so that living and dying in her motherly embrace, you may rest happily in peace.

CHAPTER FIVE

THE SCAPULAR

FLOS CARMELI

O beautiful Flower of Carmel,
most fruitful vine,
splendor of heaven,
holy and singular,
who brought forth the Son of God,
still ever remaining a pure virgin,
assist us in our necessity.
O Star of the Sea,
help and protect us.
Show us that you are our Mother.

HISTORY OF THE SCAPULAR

The scapular, derived from the Latin *scapulae*, meaning "shoulders," evolved from a kind of apron worn as part of the religious habit by monks during manual labor.

THE WORKING MONK

The first scapular was a narrow piece of cloth, less than twenty inches in width, with a large opening for the head; it hung over the monk's shoulders, down the front and back of his habit. This apron-like cloak was standard apparel for a Benedictine monk, as is described in the *Rule of St. Benedict*—the sixth-century monastic code attributed to Benedict of Nursia, patriarch of monasticism in the Latin West. The scapular was later adopted by other religious orders, such as the Dominicans and the Carmelites.

A MINIATURE HABIT

The scapular was introduced to devout laity in the thirteenth century with the formation of confraternities and third orders of penance— groups of lay persons who associated themselves with a religious order of monks, imitating the spirit of the order by practices of prayer and poverty. As a token of the person's participation in the order, it became customary for the monks to present the lay person with a scapular of the same color as the religious habits, to signify the garment worn by the order. The *New Catholic Encyclopedia* explains:

> The scapular with the rest of the habit of which it is a part, keeps before the mind of the individual religious what his order represents—its ideals, traditions, and the holiness of life achieved by many, perhaps, who have been clothed in the same uniform. As part of a uniform it is also a sign of a special bond of charity that unites those who wear and have worn it.

However, this symbolic scapular was different in form than the cloak of earlier times. It usually consisted of two pieces of cloth connected by strings or tape over the person's shoulder. One piece of cloth was to be worn on the chest; the other on the back.

THE SMALL SCAPULAR

The scapular was further reduced in the sixteenth century when what was known as the "small scapular" came into use by laity. These scapulars—consisting of two pieces of cloth that were no bigger than two-inch squares—were worn by tertiaries of third orders, but also by lay persons who participated in the prayers and practices of a certain order but did not observe the rule of a third order or confraternity. Again, the *New Catholic Encyclopedia* explains:

> The small scapular given to tertiaries or oblates is the sign of their admission into a kind of fellowship with the religious of an order and is meant to encourage their participation in the prayer, activities, and spirit of the order. Moreover, it is a pledge of some measure of participation in the merits of the order.

Unlike the third order scapular, which was usually plain and simple, the small scapular was often embroidered with the image of Mary, a saint, or an object of special devotion. These elaborate pieces of cloth came to represent different monastic orders and confraternities as types of emblems.

THE BROWN SCAPULAR

The Scapular of Our Lady of Mount Carmel— or the Brown Scapular—is primarily responsible for certain claims regarding the spiritual benefits gained by wearing the scapular. The reason for this dates back to 1251, when, according to Carmelite legend, the Blessed Virgin appeared to Saint Simon Stock, a Carmelite, at Aylesford in Kent, England. In this vision, she showed him a brown scapular, and declared that whoever wore it devoutly would be assured of eternal salvation. She made this scapular the sign of her protection.

However, the promise attributed to the scapular in this vision presents some theological problems, and therefore, must be understood in conformity with the teaching of the Church regarding the uncertainty of salvation. As with religious medals, it is wrong to attribute magical efficacy to the scapular itself; the scapular is only a channel of grace in so far as it disposes the effects of the sacraments. It is a symbol that recalls the believer to his or her faith. As explained in the pamphlet *The Scapular of Our Lady of Mount Carmel* published by the National Shrine of Our Lady of Mount Carmel:

> The Carmelite Scapular is not a magical charm to protect you; an automatic guarantee of salvation; or an excuse for not living up to the demands of the Christian life. . . . [It] is a sign of Christian faith and commitment; it points to a renewed hope of encountering God in eternal life with the help of Mary's protection and intercession.

THEOLOGY OF THE SCAPULAR

Among the symbolic meanings attached to the scapular is that of the yoke of Christ.

YOKE OF CHRIST

Because it was first worn as part of a monk's religious habit during manual labor, the scapular was thought to be a kind of cross carried on the shoulders. To wear the scapular meant to follow Christ and to take up one's cross; it became a symbol of the life of penance and poverty.

THE SPIRITUALITY OF AN ORDER

Scapulars, as mentioned earlier, also began to symbolize the particular spiritualities of the religious orders that they represented. For example, the Brown Scapular symbolized the special dedication of Carmelites to the Blessed Virgin and expressed the Order's trust in her motherly protection. The Scapular of Our Lady of Mount Carmel became a sign of Mary; to this day, it represents the desire of those who wear it to be like Mary in her commitment to Christ and to others.

THE BROWN SCAPULAR
ITS SPIRITUAL MEANING

The Brown Scapular finds its roots in the traditions of the Carmelite Order, which has seen it as a sign of Mary's motherly protection. It has a centuries-old spiritual meaning approved by the Church:

■ It is a symbol of Mary's motherly love for us.

■ It stands for a commitment to follow Jesus as Mary did. She is the perfect model of all the disciples of Christ.

■ It leads us into the family of Carmel, a community of religious men and women, which has existed in the Church for over eight centuries; it links us with the contemplative and prophetic spirituality of Carmel; and it calls on us to live out the ideal of this religious family—an intimate friendship with God in prayer.

■ It reminds us of the example of the saints of Carmel, with whom we establish a close bond as brothers and sisters to one another in Christ.

■ It is an expression of our belief that we will meet God in eternal life, aided by the intercession and prayer of Mary.

—The Scapular of Our Lady of Mount Carmel

THE SCAPULAR TODAY

Although as a devotion the use of scapulars, and especially the Brown Scapular, is far less popular than it was before the Second Vatican Council, scapulars exist today as legitimate sacramentals. Again according to the *Constitution on the Sacred Liturgy*, the scapular and other sacramentals are "sacred signs which bear a resemblance to the sacraments. They signify effects . . . which are obtained through the Church's intercession" (*Constitution on the Sacred Liturgy*, no. 60).

There are nearly twenty scapulars for devotional use. Among the most popular are the Brown Scapular, the Scapular of the Holy Trinity, the Scapular of Our Lady of the Seven Dolors, the Scapular of the Passion, and the Scapular of the Immaculate Conception.

RECEIVING THE SCAPULAR

Like religious medals, scapulars are given for wearing in a ceremony of investiture and enrollment. Once a person is invested with a scapular, he or she may replace it with a scapular medal, provided that the medal represents the Sacred Heart on one side and Our Lady on the other.

CHAPTER SIX

LITURGY OF
THE HOURS

*The Prophet says, "Seven times a day
have I praised you" (Psalm 119:164).
We will fulfill this sacred number of
seven if we satisfy our obligations of
service at Lauds, Prime, Terce, Sext,
None, Vespers, and Compline, for it
was of these hours during the day that
he said, "Seven times a day I have
praised you."*

—The Rule of Saint Benedict

HISTORY OF THE DIVINE OFFICE

The Liturgy of the Hours, also known as the Divine Office, is one of the oldest devotions, reaching back to the Jewish tradition before the birth of Christ.

THE JEWISH SYNAGOGUE

The origin of the Christian Liturgy of the Hours is found in the liturgy of the Jewish synagogue, which consists of three gatherings: the morning service (*Shaharit*); the afternoon service (*Minhah*); and the evening service (*Arvit*).

Jesus and his apostles attended the communal prayer of the synagogue, as is recorded in the New Testament, and it is probable that the earliest Christian communities continued to participate in Jewish services until the early second century, when the Jewish Christians officially broke off from the Jewish community.

As these first Christians separated from the older tradition, they instituted a routine of daily prayer similar to that of their ancestors. Early Christian writings indicate a firm tradition of hours of prayer, and gatherings devoted to sermons and reflection.

THE MONASTIC AND CATHEDRAL OFFICE

With the granting of religious freedom to Christians by the Roman Emperor Constantine in 313, two types of daily community prayer emerged: the monastic Office and the cathedral Office.

The monastic Office consisted of a rigorous routine of communal prayer throughout the day and night. Although differing from one monastic order to the next, the most common times or hours of prayer were: Matins, Lauds (Morning Prayer), Prime, Terce (9 a.m.), Sext (12 p.m.), None (3 p.m.), Vespers (Evening Prayer), and Compline.

In contrast to the monastic Office, the cathedral Office consisted of a much lighter prayer routine, with only two primary hours: Morning Prayer and Evening Prayer. Moreover, the hours of the cathedral Office were shorter, including fewer psalms.

These two Offices eventually converged, becoming one, and the number of hours—Matins, Lauds, Prime, Terce, Sext, None, Vespers, and Compline—became set sometime in the Middle Ages. However, the unified Office became more the prayer of the religious, because the rigorous routine could not be practiced by laity without much difficulty.

DEVELOPMENT OF THE BREVIARY

Sometime in the twelfth century, the Breviary—a distinct liturgical book containing the prayers of the Office—came into being. This book, created by mendicant orders to assist their members in daily prayer on their travels, allowed the Office to be said privately and at the convenience of the priest. Thus, it contributed to the privatization and clericalization of the Liturgy of the Hours that endured another four centuries.

REFORMS OF VATICAN II

Although there were subsequent attempts to revise the Breviary, the structure and content of the Office did not change much until Vatican II. In chapter four of the *Constitution on the Sacred Liturgy* (*Sacrosanctum Concilium*), the revised Liturgy of the Hours is presented. Among other reforms of the Breviary are these:

1) The psalms are distributed over four weeks instead of one.
2) The lectionary has been expanded.
3) The Liturgy of the Hours may be officially observed by any gathering of Christians, whether or not a priest or deacon is present.

REVISION OF THE DIVINE OFFICE
ACCORDING TO VATICAN II

Since the purpose of the office is to sanctify the day, the traditional sequence of the hours is to be restored so that, as far as possible, they may again become also in fact what they have been in name. At the same time account must be taken of the conditions of modern life in which those who are engaged in apostolic work must live.

Therefore, in the revision of the office these norms are to be observed:

(a) By the venerable tradition of the universal Church, Lauds as morning prayer, and Vespers as evening prayer, are the two hinges on which the daily office turns. They must be considered the chief hours and are to be celebrated as such.

(b) Compline is to be drawn up so as suitably to mark the close of the day.

(c) The hour called Matins, although it should retain the character of nocturnal prayer when recited in choir, shall be so adapted that it may be recited at any hour of the day, and it shall be made up of fewer psalms and longer readings.

(d) The hour of Prime is to be suppressed.

(e) In choir the minor hours of Terce, Sect, and None are to be observed. Outside of choir it will be lawful to select any one of the three most suited to the time of the day.

So that it may be possible in practice to observe the course of the hours proposed . . . the psalms are no longer to be distributed throughout one week but through a longer period of time.

As regards to the readings, the following points shall be observed:

(a) Readings from sacred scripture shall be so arranged that the riches of the divine word may be easily accessible in more abundant measure;

(b) Readings taken from the works of the fathers, doctors, and ecclesiastical writers shall be better selected;

(c) The accounts of the martyrdom or lives of the saints are to be made historically accurate.

So that the day may be truly sanctified and that the hours themselves may be recited with spiritual advantage, it is best that each of them be prayed at the time which corresponds most closely with its true canonical time.

—*Sacrosanctum Concilium*, no. 88-89, 91-92, 94

THEOLOGY OF THE DIVINE OFFICE

The Liturgy of the Hours is a communal celebration, a prayer of praise and thanksgiving. In the offering of praise to God at different hours, a person sanctifies his or her entire day.

THEOLOGY OF PRAISE

The theological significance of the Office is found in this praise and worship to God. As the *Constitution on the Sacred Liturgy* explains, by offering praise to God, a community shares in the greatest honor of the Church:

> The divine office, in keeping with ancient Christian tradition, is so devised that the whole course of the day and night is made holy by the praise of God. Therefore, when this wonderful song of praise is correctly celebrated . . . it is truly the voice of the Bride herself addressed to her Bridegroom. It is the very prayer which Christ himself together with his Body addresses to the Father.
>
> Hence, all who take part in the divine office are not only performing a duty for the Church, they are also sharing in what is the greatest honor for Christ's Bride. (*Constitution on the Sacred Liturgy*, no. 84-85)

ELEMENTS OF THE DIVINE OFFICE
UNITED STATES CATHOLIC CONFERENCE

Following are the elements used throughout the Liturgy of the Hours, which form its basic content.

- *Opening Hymn*. After a brief introductory verse to the hour, an appropriate hymn is sung. In addition to providing a fitting introduction to the prayer of the hour, the hymn also serves to focus the time of the day, the feast, and/or the season.

- *Psalmody*. The primary element, and the one that in a sense forms the superstructure of the Liturgy of the Hours, is the psalmody. The 150 psalms, inspired like the rest of the Bible, express the complete array of human emotions so that when prayed, it is not difficult to insert oneself in the place of the psalmist.

- *Canticles*. In addition to the psalms used throughout the Office, two of the hours include the use of canticles either from the New Testament or the Hebrew Scriptures. In Morning Prayer a canticle from the Hebrew Scriptures is placed between the two psalms; in Evening Prayer a New Testament canticle (from the epistles or the Book of Revelation) follows the two psalms. The canticle in Evening Prayer is so located as to maintain the traditional order of the New Testament texts following those selected from the Old Testament.

- *Readings*. In addition to the psalms and canticles taken from the scriptures, the Office includes and gives special place to selected readings from the Bible. Although the largest amount of scripture reading is assigned to the Office of the Readings, brief selections are, nevertheless, offered in each of the various hours. This allows for a considerable variety of texts taken from all parts of the Bible, except the gospels, to be included in the daily Office.

- *Intercessions.* In both Morning Prayer and Evening Prayer an addition has been made allowing for formal prayers of petition on the part of the community. In Morning Prayer the petitions take on the form of consecrating or commending the day to God; the intercessions at Evening Prayer are for the various needs of the Church and the world—not unlike the General Intercessions used in the liturgy of the word within the celebration of the Eucharist.

- *The Lord's Prayer and Concluding Prayer.* In the hinge hours of the Office (Morning Prayer and Evening Prayer) the intercessions are followed by the Lord's Prayer—the Church's prayer for its daily needs—said in common by all present. . . . The final prayer of all the hours is a collect similar to the Opening Prayer at Mass, corresponding to the day, the hour, the feast, or season of celebration.

- *Dismissal.* The various hours of the Office are concluded either with a formal dismissal (Morning Prayer and Evening Prayer) consisting of a blessing and dismissal, or in the case of the other hours with the brief conclusion: "Let us praise the Lord. And give him thanks."

TIMES OF PRAYER
UNITED STATES CATHOLIC CONFERENCE

In the revised Office there are basically five hours or times of prayer during the course of the day:

■ *Morning Prayer*. This is the first of the two hinge hours of the Office. Considered as one of the chief hours of the day, it is to be celebrated as a means of sanctifying the morning. Calling to mind new beginnings—light, day, work—the community is reminded of the mystery of Christ's resurrection.

■ *Daytime Prayer*. The Church presents three hours under the title of Daytime Prayer (Midmorning, Midday, Midafternoon). Normally only one of these is used, with the selection dependent on the time one chooses to pray. This use of Daytime Prayer is a continuation of the ancient tradition of maintaining formal prayer in the midst of one's daily work.

■ *Evening Prayer*. This is the second of the two hinge hours of the Office. It is celebrated in the evening, when the day is almost over. "We recall the redemption by this prayer, which we direct 'like incense before God,' and in which 'the lifting up of our hand' becomes 'an evening sacrifice'" (*General Instruction of the Liturgy of the Hours*, 39). At the setting of the sun the community directs its hopes to Christ, the light that never ends.

■ *Night Prayer.* This is the last hour of the Office, prayed at night before retiring for the day. In addition to the other elements of the Office, it includes appropriately a very brief examination of conscience not unlike the form used in the introductory rites of the Eucharist. It concludes, according to ancient tradition, with a hymn to Mary.

■ *Office of Readings.* The longest hour of prayer within the Liturgy of the Hours, the Office of the Readings, may be prayed at any time of the day, depending on circumstance. Consisting mainly of readings from the scriptures and Church writings, it provides the occasion for prayerful spiritual reading along an ancient pattern devised by the Church for the spiritual good of its members.

LITURGY OF THE HOURS TODAY

It was the intention of Vatican II to make the Liturgy of the Hours the prayer of the *entire* Church, not just of the religious. The purpose of this devotion today is to foster the prayer life of the community, as Jeffrey Vanderwilt describes in the *Encyclopedia of Catholicism*:

> The Liturgy of the Hours, when properly prayed and celebrated, nurtures the deeper intuitions that the value of incessant prayer instills: the sacramentality of time and the joyful expectation of the establishment of God's dominion among humankind. The Liturgy of the Hours also inspires among Christians the performance of daily deeds of charity and justice. Finally, the practice of daily prayer in the company of others delivers Christians from the need to devise ways to express their own needs and desires to God. Alternatively and at its best, the public prayer of the Church delivers humanity to a God who calls people out of themselves and into the mystery of infinite love.

We can see that the Liturgy of the Hours is alive and well in the prayer life of today's Church in reading such journals as Kathleen Norris' *Cloister Walk*, about her discovering monastic liturgy and the beauty of the psalms.

KATHLEEN NORRIS
THE CLOISTER WALK

Not having been to church for some twenty years following high school, I rediscovered the psalms by accident, through my unexpected attraction to Benedictine liturgy, of which the psalms are the mainstay. . . . As I began to immerse myself in monastic liturgy, I found that I was also immersed in poetry and was grateful to find that the poetic nature of the psalms, their constant movement between the mundane and the exalted, means, as British Benedictine Sebastian Moore has said, that "God behaves in the psalms in ways he is not allowed to behave in systematic theology," and also that the images of the psalms, "rough-hewn from earthy experience, [are] absolutely different from formal prayer."

I also discovered, in two nine-month sojourns with the St. John's community, that as Benedictine prayer rolls on, as daily as marriage and washing dishes, it tends to sweep away the concerns of systematic theology and church doctrine. All of that is there, as a kind of scaffolding, but the psalms demand engagement, they ask you to read them with your whole self, praying, as St. Benedict says, "in such a way that our minds are in harmony with our voices."

CHAPTER SEVEN

EUCHARISTIC ADORATION

In silence,
To be there before you, Lord, that's all,
To shut the eyes of my body,
To shut the eyes of my soul,
And to be still and silent,
To expose myself to you who are there,
    exposed to me.
To be there before you,
    the Eternal Presence . . .

—Michel Quoist

HISTORY OF EUCHARISTIC ADORATION

Eucharistic adoration is defined in the *Encyclopedia of Catholicism* as:

> A devotion centered on worshipping Christ as
> Divine Lord and Savior in the consecrated bread
> (and wine). Though such adoration is expressed
> in the liturgy itself, this term has come to
> designate nonliturgical worship, usually involv-
> ing exposition of the Blessed Sacrament. Many
> persons also have engaged in such adoration
> privately through visits to the Blessed Sacrament.

In this chapter, I mean eucharistic adoration to include all kinds of eucharistic devotions, "nonliturgical religious practices centered on Christ's presence to the Church in the reserved Sacrament" (*Encyclopedia of Catholicism*), including exposition of the Blessed Sacrament, Benediction, and eucharistic processions and visits.

CONSECRATION OF THE BREAD

Eucharistic adoration originated with the elevation of the host at the moment of consecration in the Mass, the reservation of the Eucharist for public view, and the celebration of the Feast of the Corpus Christi. These practices developed sometime beginning in the late twelfth century as persons began to perceive the Eucharist in a realistic way, replacing a more symbolic understanding of earlier years.

The emergence of eucharistic devotions during this time were also the result of an increasing desire among the faithful to look at and contemplate Christ in the consecrated bread and wine. Eucharistic devotion was so valued in popular piety that, at least for some time, it seemed to replace the liturgical celebration of the Eucharist in the Mass as the most important form of worship.

INTEGRATION WITH THE MASS

Beginning with Vatican II, the Church has attempted to reintegrate nonliturgical eucharistic adoration with the Mass. Contemporary teaching, as the *Encyclopedia of Catholicism* explains, understands eucharistic devotions as continuations of the liturgical celebration:

> [Eucharistic] devotions are seen as prolongations of thanksgiving, of interior communion with one's saving Lord, of prayer for the Church and world, all of which are celebrated and actualized in the Eucharistic Liturgy.

THEOLOGY OF EUCHARISTIC ADORATION

Eucharistic adoration turns the attention of the
faithful to the Mass, the eucharistic sacrifice,
which is "the source and summit of the whole
Christian life" (*Lumen Gentium*, no. 11). That is
the essence of its theology.

PRESENCE OF CHRIST

In proper context, eucharistic adoration makes
us more aware, or leads us to a deeper understanding, of the presence of Christ in the sacrament of
the Eucharist. When we concentrate on the
Blessed Sacrament—in the liturgical celebration of
the Eucharist at Mass, or as a nonliturgical
devotion—we meditate on Christ Crucified. The
theological purpose of eucharistic adoration, then,
exists in the remembrance, celebration, and
affirmation of the Paschal Mystery, our Christian
story of redemption.

Once again, I use the words of Karl Rahner to
articulate the spiritual value of our devotion. In his
prayer "The Sacrament of the Altar," Rahner
beautifully articulates this remembrance,
celebration, and affirmation of the Christian story
that is at the core of eucharistic adoration.

KARL RAHNER
THE SACRAMENT OF THE ALTAR

We kneel, Lord, before the Sacrament on the altars of Your holy Church, before the Sacrament of God's new and eternal covenant with the race of all the redeemed. We lift up our eyes to You, Lord, who are present among us in flesh and blood, body and soul, in divinity and humanity. . . .

We kneel, Lord, before Your Sacrament, which unites us to You, to You the Son and the Eternal Word of the Father, to You, the Son of Man. When we eat this bread, we remain in You and You in us. When we receive You, You transform us into a part of Yourself, and faith, hope, and charity grow. When we have part in You, the Bread of Life and pledge of glory to come, we the many are one body; then either we eat judgment on our own selfishness or we receive the power of love, which frees, unites and includes everything.

When we, as one holy community, raise You up as the sacrifice of the new covenant, when we receive You, then we show Your death until You come again, and You renew with us and in us the mystery of Your death. We are baptized into Your death. As often as we receive this Sacrament we acknowledge the mystery of Your death, which is life. You are in truth our bread, You who came among us in Your own Word, and You are in truth the Word in which the Father speaks to himself all truth for ever and ever. . . .

In the Sacrament of the Altar Your humanity is the pledge which unites us with Your divinity. Your humanity touches us and consecrates us. So may we, through this sacrament, become what we are: men, honest and true in body and soul, men in whom the presence of Your grace can find a symbol which will become effective for those whom we have to serve.

Be for us who worship and receive You as the hidden, silent, sacrificed God of our life and death, a pledge of eternal life: the life of truth and of boundless freedom, the life of light and of undimmed brightness, the life in which we shall be blissfully consumed in adoration of the unsearchable God, the life in which all creatures will celebrate their blessed surrender to the Father, and God will become all in all.

What we enact in the Church's sacrificial rite, in our adoration of this Sacrament, in the receiving of Your Body and Blood, will, by Your grace, always be enacted and celebrated in the sacred enactment of our own life, in its daily routines and in its climaxes, in life and in death.

—*Prayers for a Lifetime*

EUCHARISTIC ADORATION TODAY

As mentioned briefly before, the Church today discourages the devotion of eucharistic adoration done in isolation from the liturgy. Vatican II's post-conciliar document *Instruction on the Worship of the Eucharistic Mystery* describes this necessary relationship between liturgical and nonliturgical eucharistic devotions:

> In determining the form of such [Eucharistic] devotions, account should be taken of the regulations of the Second Vatican Council concerning the relationship to be maintained between the liturgy and other, nonliturgical, celebrations. (*Eucharisticum Mysterium*, no. 58)

KINDS OF EUCHARISTIC DEVOTION

Among the forms of eucharistic devotion practiced today are: exposition of the Blessed Sacrament, in which the consecrated host is displayed in a monstrance upon the altar or tabernacle for the worship of the faithful; Benediction, usually following exposition and adoration of the Blessed Sacrament, including a blessing of the people with the Sacrament; and eucharistic processions and visits, in which the faithful make private visits to the Blessed Sacrament, usually laid in the tabernacle, as a form of special reverence and adoration.

SECOND TO THE MASS

In an effort to secure the status of the Mass as the most important form of Christian worship and to prevent the exaggerated value of nonliturgical devotions that has occurred in the past, the *Constitution on the Sacred Liturgy* asserts the primordial place of the liturgy among other devotions:

> [Liturgical] devotions should be so drawn up that they harmonize with the liturgical seasons, accord with the sacred liturgy, are in some way derived from it, and lead the people to it, since in fact the liturgy by its very nature is far superior to any of them. (*Constitution on the Sacred Liturgy*, no. 13)

CHAPTER EIGHT

DEVOTION TO THE SAINTS

Veneration of the saints is . . . one of the most important fruits of brotherly love. . . . Just as our love of Christ cannot be separated from our fraternal love, so it would be wrong to regard veneration of the saints as superfluous to Christian worship. . . . Worship of the saints, considered as an aspect of general worship rather than as a particular devotional practice, is a duty for every Christian.

—Edward Schillebeeckx

HISTORY OF DEVOTION TO THE SAINTS

Saints are defined, in the strictest sense, by the *Encyclopedia of Catholicism* as:

> Those officially recognized (canonized) by the Church as persons who have lived a holy life, who now share in the Beatific Vision (i.e., face-to-face experience of the presence of God), and who may be publicly venerated by the faithful.

Although anyone who enjoys eternal life with God is considered a saint, this chapter is concerned primarily with the devotion to and veneration of the saints as defined above.

CULT OF THE MARTYRS

Devotion to the saints is identified in its origins with the cult of the martyrs and the veneration of the original disciples of Jesus. Christians of the first two centuries praised and tried to imitate these persons, the first of the saints. By the third century, early Christian writings already suggest an invocation to saints for special graces from God.

In the centuries that followed, confessors—persons who suffered for the faith—hermits, monks, virgins, and finally holy persons who led exceptional Christian lives were added to the list. Like the martyrs and disciples, these saints were honored on their anniversaries, and churches were put under their protection. In addition, legends of their lives were published and celebrated.

A FLOWERING OF SAINTS

In the Middle Ages, the list of venerated persons grew to enormous proportions, creating a flowering of popular devotions to the saints. Among these practices were pilgrimages, widespread honoring of relics, the naming of patron saints, the celebration of civic festivals with liturgical feasts, and compilations of legends of the saints.

As a result of exaggerated practices with regard to devotion to saints, Church authorities established a process whereby a bishop—after reviewing the life of the prospective saint—decided who was and who was not to be canonized; however, it was not long after that formal approval for canonization came only from the pope.

VENERATION OF THE SAINTS

The protestors of the Reformation became increasingly uncomfortable with the veneration of saints because, according to them, saintly intercession suggested that Christ is not the unique mediator between God and humans; they found these devotions to take away from devotion to Christ. However, the Council of Trent (1545-1563) reaffirmed the Church's teaching regarding the intercession of the saints, and encouraged invocation to them by the faithful.

THREE KINDS OF WORSHIP

Although the Church affirms intercession and encourages invocation of the saints, Catholic doctrine makes a clear distinction between the veneration given to saints—*dulia*, Greek for "service or veneration"—and the adoration or worship that is afforded to God alone—*latria*, meaning "worship." (Veneration of Mary, *hyperdulia*, "more than veneration," is a sort of glorified *dulia*.)

By distinguishing between *dulia* and *latria*, the Church teaches that we pray only to God, and that the special graces or blessings bestowed on us come from God through the saint's intercession. Moreover, honor given to the saints is honor given to God because holiness is only possible with the gift of God's grace. Thus, devotion to the saints is praise and glory directed to God.

FAVORITE PATRON SAINTS

—*Saint Francis of Assisi*
  Patron of animals and birds

—*Saint Jude Thaddeus*
  Patron of lost causes

—*Saint Thérèse of Lisieux*
  Patroness of missionaries and florists

—*Saint Anthony of Padua*
  Patron of lost articles

—*Saint Margaret of Antioch*
  Patroness of pregnancy and birth

—*Saint Joseph*
  Patron of fatherhood and families

—*Saint Mary*
  Patroness of motherhood

—*Saint Monica*
  Patronness of the widowed

—*Saint Valentine*
  Patron of love

—*Saint Patrick*
  Patron of Ireland

—*Saint Cecilia*
  Patroness of musicians

—*Saint Martin de Porres*
Patron of racial harmony and social justice

—*Saint Nicholas*
Patron of children

—*Saint Geneviève*
Patroness of disasters

—*Saint Michael the Archangel*
Patron of soldiers

—*Saint Thomas the Apostle*
Patron of architects and builders

—*Saint Mary Magdalene*
Patroness of repentant sinners

—*Saint Thomas Aquinas*
Patron of students and scholars

—*Saint Clare of Assisi*
Patroness of television

—*Saint Blaise*
Patron of sore throats

—*Saint Teresa of Ávila*
Patronness of Spain and headaches

—*Saint Frances Cabrini*
Patroness of immigrants

—*Saint Vincent de Paul*
Patron of charitable giving

THEOLOGY OF DEVOTION TO THE SAINTS

Lawrence Cunningham defines saints in his book *The Meaning of Saints* as:

> A person so grasped by a religious vision that it becomes central to his or her life in a way that radically changes the person and leads others to glimpse the value of the vision.

INSTRUMENTS OF GOD

The saints, as Christian role models, are finely tuned instruments of God, through which divine inspiration produces majestic sound. They are pieces of clay that remain so malleable throughout their lives that God is able to nearly finish the masterpiece he intended upon creating them. Saints live for and by their mission, or vision, as Cunningham would say. Hans Urs von Balthasar explains in his article "The Saints as Theme of Theology" the uncompromising obedience of all saints to a certain mission.

> The most important thing about great saints is their mission, a new charism bestowed on the church by the Holy Spirit. The person who possesses it and bears it, is only the servant of the Spirit, a servant who is weak and unprofitable

even to the point of the most sublime achieve-
ments in whom the luminous quality is not the
person, but the testimony, the task, the office. . . .
All saints . . . realize the deficiency in their
service to the mission. . . . The chief thing about
them is not the heroic personal achievement, but
the resolute obedience with which they have
given themselves over to being slaves to a
mission and understand their entire existence
only as a function of and protective covering for
this mission. (*The von Balthasar Reader*)

EXEMPLARS OF CHRIST

Because saints are exemplars of Christ, by
devotion to them we are able to better understand
and appreciate the saving mystery of our Lord's
life, death, and resurrection. Harvey Egan, an
American contemporary and interpreter of Karl
Rahner, argues this point in his article on
mysticism and theology in which he discusses
Rahner's astonishing pronouncement that "the
devout Christian of the future will be a mystic":

The most significant reason for focusing upon the
important Christian mystics and saints as an
indispensable source of theology is the depth and
clarity of their experience of God and the
dramatic way in which they have lived the
mysteries of the life, death, and resurrection of
Jesus Christ. (*Theology and Discovery*)

HANS URS VON BALTHASAR
CHURCH—COMMUNITY OF SAINTS

■ The extent to which the saints—those who attempt to take seriously their sanctification by the holy triune God and to respond to it—are able in their community to be, to live, to work, and to suffer for one another can only begin to be realized when one has grasped the principle which welds them together into the unity of the community of the church: the unity of the triune God manifested in the self-giving of Christ and poured out in the Holy Spirit. For this unity is nothing other than pure being-for-one-another.

■ The communion of saints cannot be a closed circle of those who exchange their profits among themselves, in much the same manner in which [business] firms amalgamate, in order to get a higher yield on their capital. The communion of saints can only be an open circle of those who "give without counting the cost," who let their light shine into the world without looking for its reflection. That alone is *agape*, *caritas*; only so did Christ pour himself out on the cross and in the Eucharist. And consequently, it is not possible to set limits to the comprehensiveness and effectiveness of this open circle.

- There is perhaps no more comforting truth about the church than that in it there is a community, a communion of saints. For, on the one hand, this means that there is a continually overflowing richness on which all the poor may draw; it is also called the treasure of the church. It is precisely the same as the incalculable fruitfulness of those who offer themselves and all that they have to God to dispose of for the sake of the brotherhood and sisterhood. Real power goes forth from them; they are not spared by love (Romans 8:32) but are rigorously shared. . . . This excess which comes to us makes us poor and humble, for we sense precisely that we can only draw on such richness in the same spirit in which it has been given. . . . The idea of the communion of saints inspires no little caution in us. On the other hand, it also exhorts us not to underestimate the fruitfulness which has been given us by God.

—The von Balthasar Reader

DEVOTION TO THE SAINTS TODAY

Like all of our Catholic devotions, devotion to the saints has changed significantly since the Second Vatican Council. To discourage exaggerated practices of this devotion in isolation from the Church's teachings, veneration of the saints—according to the *Dogmatic Constitution on the Church*—has been tied in more closely with worship of Christ and with the liturgical life of the Church:

> Every authentic witness of love, indeed, offered by us to those who are in heaven tends to and terminates in Christ, "the crown of all saints," and through him in God who is wonderful in his saints and is glorified in them.
>
> It is especially in the sacred liturgy that our union with the heavenly Church is best realized; in the liturgy, through the sacramental signs, the power of the Holy Spirit acts on us, and with community rejoicing we celebrate together the praise of the divine majesty. . . . When, then, we celebrate the eucharistic sacrifice we are most closely united to the worship of the heavenly Church; when in the fellowship of communion we honor and remember the glorious Mary ever virgin, St. Joseph, the holy apostles and martyrs and all the saints. (*Dogmatic Constitution on the Church*, no. 50)

KENNETH L. WOODWARD
MAKING SAINTS

Only God makes saints. Still, it is up to us to tell their stories. That, in the end, is the only rationale for the process of "making saints." What sort of story befits a saint? Not tragedy, certainly. Comedy comes closer to capturing the playfulness of genuine holiness and the supreme logic of a life lived in and through God. An element of suspense is also required: until the story is over, one can never be certain of the outcome. True saints are the last people on earth to presume their own salvation—in this life or in the next.

My own hunch is that the story of a saint is always a love story. It is a story of a God who loves, and of the beloved who learns how to reciprocate and share that "harsh and dreadful love."

It is a story that includes misunderstanding, deception, betrayal, concealment, reversal, and revelation of character. It is, if the saints are to be trusted, our story. But to be a saint is not to be a solitary lover. It is to enter into deeper communion with everyone and everything that exists.

CHAPTER NINE

DEVOTION TO THE SACRED HEART

The devotion to the Sacred Heart of Jesus is nothing more than an exercise of love toward our loving Savior. Therefore the principal object of this devotion, the spiritual object of this devotion, is the love with which the heart of Jesus is inflamed toward all.

—Saint Alphonsus Liguori

HISTORY OF THE SACRED HEART

Although tradition often situates the origin of devotion to the Sacred Heart around the year 1000, contemporary theology is finding scriptural and patristic sources of the devotion.

THE FOUNTAIN OF LIVING WATER

The image of the pierced Heart of Jesus from which streams of living water flow is most clearly seen in the Gospel of John, although hints of this Christian symbol first appear in the Hebrew scriptures. In John 7:37-39 is written:

> On the last day of the festival, the great day, while Jesus was standing there, he cried out, "Let anyone who is thirsty come to me, and let the one who believes in me drink. As the scripture has said, 'Out of the believer's heart shall flow rivers of living water.'"

Some of the early Church Fathers interpreted the above verse to say "living water streaming forth from the heart of Christ." This passage together with John 19:33-37—"One of the soldiers pierced his side . . . and at once blood and water came out" (John 19:34)—forms the earliest picture of the Sacred Heart.

PERSONAL DEVOTION TO JESUS' HEART

Patristic teaching regarding the Heart of Jesus and the wound in his side as sources of grace eventually developed into a more personal devotion, directed to the Heart of Jesus as a symbol of Christ's redemptive love. Personal devotion to the Heart of Jesus is evident in the writings of Saint Anselm and Saint Bernard.

Concentrating on the Heart of Jesus became popular in the devotional life of the religious by the Middle Ages because of the strong emphasis on Christ's Passion during this time. Personal devotion to the Sacred Heart was further encouraged by such mystics as Saint Bonaventure and Saint Gertrude the Great.

PROPAGATION OF THE DEVOTION

In the centuries that followed, devotion to the Sacred Heart became widespread among the laity, promoted by the Carthusians and taken up by the *Devotio Moderna* (Latin for "Modern Devotion"), a movement of spiritual renewal originating in fourteenth-century Holland that emphasized the inner life of the individual. The Sisters of the Visitation and the newly founded Society of Jesus were ardent advocates of the devotion, as well.

SAINT MARGARET MARY ALACOQUE

Although Saint John Eudes (1601-1680) was named teacher and apostle of the cult of the Sacred Heart by Pope Pius X, this devotion was most promoted and popularized by Saint Margaret Mary Alacoque (1647-1690). The private revelations made to her at Paray-le-Monial from 1673-1675 considerably shaped the practices of devotion to the Sacred Heart, especially regarding acts of reparation and consecration that are a part of today's devotion.

It was at Paray-le-Monial that the practice of enthroning an image of the Sacred Heart in the home began, in 1907, with the formation of the Enthronement Crusade. Inspired by the requests and promises of the Sacred Heart revealed to Saint Margaret Mary more than two and a quarter centuries back, the crusade promoted this practice in all parts of the world.

CHURCH APPROVAL

In 1856, Pius IX extended the Feast of the Sacred Heart, which had previously been celebrated only by the bishops of Poland, to the universal Church. The feast is celebrated on the Friday after Corpus Christi.

THEOLOGY OF THE SACRED HEART

Devotion to the Sacred Heart of Jesus points to the threefold love of Christ: human love, sensible and spiritual love (infused love), and divine love. It is, as the *Encyclopedia of Catholicism* explains:

> A form of devotion to Jesus Christ as the Word of God Incarnate, consisting of veneration of his physical heart, united to his divinity, as the symbol of his redemptive love.

SYMBOL OF THE HEART

Devotion to the Sacred Heart distinguishes itself from other forms of devotion to Christ, the Second Person of the Holy Trinity, by concentrating on the physical heart of Jesus. C. J. Moell explains the theological meaning of the symbol of heart in the *New Catholic Encyclopedia*:

> The Heart of Christ is the symbol of the total love of His person. . . . Through and beyond the human heart one goes to the total love of the Word Incarnate. . . . Since the love of Christ is redemptive on each of these three levels [human, infused, and divine], the pierced Heart of Christ hanging on the cross perfectly epitomizes the whole paschal mystery of our Redemption.

SAINT ALPHONSUS LIGUORI
NOVENA TO THE SACRED HEART

First Meditation: The Amiable Heart of Jesus

O my amiable Redeemer, who could I love more than you? You are the beauty of paradise, you are the love of your Father, your heart is the throne of virtue.

Second Meditation: The Loving Heart of Jesus

O adorable heart of my Jesus, heart inflamed with the love of humanity, heart created on purpose to love them . . . do not permit me in the future, even for a single moment, to live without your love.

Third Meditation: The Heart of Jesus Christ Desires to Be Loved

My dearest Redeemer . . . give me the strength necessary to put your grace into action, and make me, from this day forward, a person who can pray from the bottom of my heart, and to repeat to you always, "My God, I love you, I love you!"

Fourth Meditation: The Sorrowful Heart of Jesus

My adorable and dearest Jesus, behold at your feet a person who has caused so much sorrow to your amiable heart. O my God, how could I wound your heart, which has loved me so much?

Fifth Meditation: The Compassionate Heart of Jesus

O compassionate heart of my Jesus, have pity on me: Most sweet Jesus, have mercy on me. . . . O my Jesus, do not cease to show your compassion toward me. I love you, and I will always love you.

Sixth Meditation: The Generous Heart of Jesus

Ah, my Jesus, you have not refused to give me your blood and your life. . . . I beseech you, O my God, teach me a perfect forgetfulness of myself.

Seventh Meditation: The Grateful Heart of Jesus

O my beloved Jesus, behold at your feet an ungrateful sinner. I have been grateful toward creatures, but to you alone I have been ungrateful; to you, who have died for me.

Eighth Meditation: The Despised Heart of Jesus

O heart of Jesus, abyss of mercy and love . . . grant me today the grace to begin to love you. Make me die to everything in myself in order that I may live only for you.

Ninth Meditation: The Faithful Heart of Jesus

O loving and faithful heart of Jesus . . . make me love you exceedingly. Make me remain faithful to you until death.

DEVOTION TO THE SACRED HEART TODAY

There are several forms of devotion to the Sacred Heart. Specific practices of today's devotion include the following:

1) Celebration of the Feast of the Sacred Heart on the Friday following the second Sunday after Pentecost (sometimes celebrated by offering reparation to the Sacred Heart as prescribed by Pius XI).

2) Devotion of the Nine Fridays (receiving the Eucharist on the first Friday of nine consecutive months).

3) Consecration to the Sacred Heart on the Feast of Christ the King (an annual renewal of Leo XIII's act of consecrating the world to the Sacred Heart in his encyclical *Annum Sacrum*).

4) Recitation of the Litany of the Sacred Heart and other prayers.

5) Adoration and Enthronement of the Sacred Heart in the home.

CHAPTER TEN

NOVENAS

NOVENA TO SAINT THÉRÈSE

Saint Thérèse, the Little Flower,
please pick me a rose
from the heavenly garden,
and send it to me
with a message of love.
Ask God to grant me the favor
I thee implore,
and tell him I will love him
each day more and more.

HISTORY OF NOVENAS

The word *novena* comes from the Latin *novem* meaning "nine." We usually refer to it as a prayer said over the course of nine days. However, the *Encyclopedia of Catholicism* defines it as:

> A public or private devotion repeated nine successive *times* . . . continuous days (nine days prior to a special feast), specific weekdays (nine Mondays), or specific days of the month (nine First Fridays).

A PERIOD OF MOURNING

The origin of this devotion is found with the nine-day period of mourning practiced by the Romans, Greeks, and other cultures of antiquity. According to their custom, on the ninth day after a death or burial, a special feast was held to commemorate the death. This pagan practice was adopted and altered by Christians, who began to say Mass for nine days after a death.

PREPARATORY NOVENAS

Devotional novenas said in preparation of a special feast first appeared in the early Middle Ages throughout France and Spain. The first of this kind was a nine-day prayer before Christmas, the number nine representing the duration of Mary's pregnancy. (A form of this ancient practice is alive today in the "O Antiphons," a series of seven antiphons that begin on December 17, nine days before Christmas.) Other devotional novenas associated with various feasts, especially those of favorite saints and special titles of Our Lady, came into practice shortly after.

NOVENAS FOR SPECIAL INTENTIONS

Novenas in honor of Our Lady and popular saints became prayers of special supplication as particular kinds of blessings began to be attributed to different saints and to Mary under specific titles. Novenas were often said to obtain healing or recovery of health, since medicine in earlier times was often of little comfort to those who suffered from various illnesses and diseases. For example, persons who had been bitten by dogs might say a novena to Saint Hubert, who was known to protect against rabies.

Throughout the following centuries novenas grew more popular, but it was not until the nineteenth century that indulgences came to be attached to them.

POPULAR NOVENAS

Novenas generally begin nine days preceding the feast with which they are associated.

—*Novena of Grace (to Saint Francis Xavier)*
  Celebrated March 12th

—*Novena to the Sacred Heart*
  Celebrated on the Friday following
  the second Sunday after Pentecost

—*Novena to the Immaculate Conception*
  Celebrated December 8th

—*Novena to the Immaculate Heart of Mary*
  Celebrated August 22nd

—*Novena to Our Mother of Perpetual Help*
  Celebrated June 27th

—*Novena to Saint Joseph*
  Celebrated March 19th

—*Novena to Saint Jude*
  Celebrated October 28th

—*Novena to Saint Thérèse*
  Celebrated October 1st

—*Novena to Our Lady of Guadalupe*
  Celebrated December 12th

THEOLOGY OF NOVENAS

The theology of novenas is found in their devotion to Mary and to the saints, as well as in their preparation for the celebration of certain liturgical feasts and solemnities.

SPIRITUAL VALUE OF REPETITION

Not only do novenas deepen our relationship with the triune God through the intercession of Mary and the saints, but they enrich our prayer life by encouraging us to pray over an extended period of time and by requiring a certain repetition of words. Describing the spiritual benefit of novenas, P. K. Meagher says in the *New Catholic Encyclopedia*:

> [A novena] is a practice that can be most serviceable to true devotion and piety. Perseverance and constancy are qualities of all good prayer, and it is well that some devotional practices should give special emphasis to them by requiring repetition on successive days over a more or less extended period of time, for this manifests and stimulates the worshiper's earnestness and fervor.

NOVENAS TODAY

Since the theological reforms of the Second
Vatican Council, there has been a strong vigilance
with regard to novenas. Novenas, more than most
Catholic practices, are seen as having a dangerous
propensity toward superstition because of the
many extraordinary effects that have been attributed to some, and because the number nine is
central to the these devotions.

However, like other forms of popular piety,
novenas are beneficial as prayer tools of the
faithful when done within the proper context—in
such a way that they "harmonize with the liturgical
seasons, accord with the sacred liturgy . . . and
lead the people to it" (*Constitution on the Sacred
Liturgy*, no. 13).

CHAPTER ELEVEN

PILGRIMAGES

We shall not cease from exploration
And the end of all our exploring
Will be to arrive where we started
And know the place for the first time.
Through the unknown, remembered gate
When the last of earth left to discover
Is that which was the beginning . . .

—*T. S. Eliot,* Four Quartets

HISTORY OF PILGRIMAGES

According to the *Encyclopedia of Catholicism*, a pilgrimage is:

> A religiously motivated journey to a specific location to visit a holy person or to commemorate a special event that occurred there. The journey to and from this special place, along with the stay, comprise the pilgrimage.

THE WAY OF SORROWS

As discussed in the chapter on the Stations of the Cross, the first pilgrimages were journeys to the Holy Land made by persons who wanted to visit the significant places along the *Via Dolorosa*, the Way of Sorrows, as a means of meditating on the pain and suffering of our Lord before his death. By the fourth century shrines were erected at these holy places, and pilgrimages to Jerusalem became popular as a devotional practice.

CELTIC SPIRITUALITY

Beginning in about the fifth century, with the influence of Saint Jerome (d. 420), pilgrimages came to be regarded among Irish monks and Celtic cultures as a form of self-isolation, a means of obtaining solitude. Celtic spirituality in its vigorous asceticism encouraged voluntary exile far from home, a fleeing of the urban environment. Throughout the following centuries, pilgrimages were also considered a form of penance imposed by the Irish for serious sins or offences committed by persons.

THE GREAT SHRINES OF EUROPE

From about the tenth century on, specific shrines became the goals or destinations of pilgrims. Especially popular were the shrines of Canterbury, Santiago, Cologne, and Rome. By the Middle Ages there were a considerable number of travelers visiting shrines throughout Europe. For many the journey was still an exercise of penance. For others the pilgrimage was a form of banishment or punishment imposed by civil authorities for violent crimes. And there eventually came to be the last group, who considered these travels a form of tourism.

By the end of the Middle Ages, pilgrimages were a central part of popular religion, especially as indulgences became attached to certain journeys, and relics—the remains of saints regarded as objects of devotion—were distributed at shrines.

THEOLOGY OF PILGRIMAGES

Persons embark on pilgrimages for several devotional purposes. As they have always been, pilgrimages are penitential exercises, a kind of reparation for sins committed. These holy travels can also be an ascetic practice, a voluntary exile away from home or a leaving behind of all worldly possessions and concerns. Persons journey as a way of seeking spiritual guidance or direction. Finally, persons make pilgrimages in petition to God for a special request, and/or in thanksgiving for a favor received.

THREE REQUISITES OF A PILGRIMAGE

According to the *Encyclopedia of Catholicism*, the following elements constitute an authentic pilgrimage:

1) The belief that God responds to prayer.
2) The conviction that God is present at holy sites.
3) The desire to make a sacred journey to a holy site.

Judged under these criteria, we could say that journeys made for any of the above reasons—for penance, as an ascetic exercise, for spiritual direction, and/or in petition or thanksgiving to God for special graces—are authentic pilgrimages.

THE INNER JOURNEY

Although we most often think of a pilgrimage as an excursion to a geographically remote location, a spiritual journey does not have to involve physical travel. The great mystics of Christian spirituality—Saint Bonaventure, Teresa of Ávila, and John of the Cross—wrote about interior ascents and descents within the soul, a kind of inner journey to find God.

The concept of an inner seeking is a popular topic in contemporary spirituality, embraced by many of today's theologians and spiritual writers.

PILGRIM CHURCH OF GOD

Our life journey can also be thought of as a kind of pilgrimage, toward a heavenly Jerusalem, or eternal life with God. Moreover, the Church is often referred to in the documents of Vatican II as the "pilgrim Church" on earth.

POPULAR PILGRIMAGE SITES

—*The Holy Land*

—*Rome, Italy (Vatican City)*

—*Lourdes, France*

—*Fatima, Portugal*

—*Medjugorje, Herzegovina*

—*Mexico City (Guadalupe), Mexico*

—*Santiago de Compostela, Spain*

—*Canterbury, England*

—*Czestochowa, Poland*

—*Assisi, Italy*

—*Knock, Ireland*

—*Walsingham, England*

—*Chartres, France*

PILGRIMAGES TODAY

Of the many popular pilgrimage sites visited by Catholics today, most are places of Marian apparitions. Lourdes, Mexico City (Guadalupe), Fatima, and Medjugorje are among the most visited, attracting millions of pilgrims each year. It is estimated that Lourdes alone attracts more than four million visitors annually.

MARIAN SHRINES

Even aside from the scenes of Marian apparitions, the majority of shrines that are visited by pilgrims—and especially those throughout Europe—are dedicated to Mary. Some Marian shrines have attracted pilgrims since Medieval Europe, such as the cathedral at Chartres, which held the relic of the tunic of Mary. Others are important for "miraculous" images or icons of Mary, such as the shrine in Poland that holds the icon of Our Lady of Czestochowa.

THE PATH TO SANTIAGO

In addition to popular Marian sites, there has been renewed interest, especially among the young, in the pilgrimage to Santiago de Compostela in Galicia, Spain. In contemporary devotional life, this medieval path has once again become a way of feeding the soul with the spirituality of the first believing community. According to tradition, the shrine of Santiago holds the relics of Saint James the Great, who is said to have evangelized Spain.

Rome and Jerusalem continue to be two of the most important pilgrimage sites today, as well, with millions of persons annually visiting both places.

CHAPTER TWELVE

ICONS AND
SACRED ART

*An icon is like a window
looking out upon eternity.
Behind its two dimensional surface
lies the garden of God,
which is beyond dimension or size.*

—Henri J. M. Nouwen,
   Behold the Beauty of the Lord

HISTORY OF ICONS AND SACRED ART

Sacred art, often used interchangeably with the
term "liturgical art," is defined by the *Encyclopedia of Catholicism* as:

> The study, design, and creation of images in
> service to Christian revelation, the human
> expression of encounter with God or the holy.

There are several types or media of sacred art,
such as icons and paintings; statuary; furnishings;
and vesture and textiles. In this chapter we'll
explore sacred art primarily as it is expressed in
icons—sacred, often portable, representations of
Christ, Mary, angels, or saints.

SACRED ART AS RELIGIOUS EDUCATION

Among the earliest purposes of sacred art was
that of religious education and faith development.
Beautiful images could (and still can) often tell the
Christian story more effectively than words. Early
Christian art portrayed persons and events of our
tradition so as to teach the faithful about the
history of Christian salvation.

As the theology of Christ's person—two
natures, human and divine, in one entity—became

more sophisticated with the christological controversies beginning in the fourth century, artists found it increasingly more difficult to paint or illustrate the Christian story to everyone's (theological) satisfaction. However, by the tenth century, religious art was again being used to instruct and edify the faithful.

THEOLOGICAL DISPUTES

Especially significant to the development of sacred art and icons was iconoclasm—the destruction of religious images in expressing strong opposition to them—which occurred during the Byzantine Empire, from about 717-843. The iconoclastic controversies of this time were, theologically speaking, a sequel to the christological controversies of earlier centuries.

At the Second Council of Nicaea (787), the controversies were resolved in favor of the use of images. Iconoclasm, however, never completely disappeared, and it resurfaced with new force at the time of the Protestant Reformation.

Like the iconoclast Byzantine emperors of the eighth century, the Reformers cleansed churches of all religious images and statues. In doing so they shifted expression of the sacred from visual media to the written and spoken word of God.

THE CHURCH AS PATRON OF ART

As a result of these theological disputes, the Church became an avid supporter of art, especially sacred art as it was (is) used toward praise of God in the liturgy. And as the Church spread throughout the globe in the centuries following the Reformation, so too did the beautiful artwork that it valued and empowered. So ardent was the financial and political support of the Church toward fine art that many of our classical masterpieces in the West are, in fact, religious art.

THE EASTERN TRADITION

In its profound appreciation of beautiful art, the Eastern tradition has promoted the use of religious imagery in popular piety throughout history and today, especially as it is used to enhance the sacred liturgy. The East regards the painting of icons to be a very important ministry within the Church—in fact prayer is essential in the painting of icons—because icons and sacred art are a central part of the Orthodox liturgy.

THEOLOGY OF ICONS AND SACRED ART

Icons are like "windows into the eternal world of revelation" (*Encyclopedia of Catholicism*). As Henri Nouwen describes, when we gaze at an icon we are "looking out upon eternity," and into the "garden of God."

MANIFESTATIONS OF THE DIVINE

Icons and religious paintings are "manifestations (epiphanies) of the divine in the human, the eternal in the temporal" (*Encyclopedia of Catholicism*). In the East especially, icons of Christ are based theologically on the Incarnation, God-Made-Man. Their devotional purpose is to point the faithful to the Image of God, the Word Incarnate, the revelation of God in Christianity as disclosed in the man of Nazareth, the God-Man Jesus Christ.

Icons of the saints are manifestations of the holy in a similar, yet unique way, as explained in the *New Catholic Encyclopedia*:

> In representing a saint the icon shares in the sanctity and glory of its prototype. It is a vessel of the grace that the saint has acquired during his life. This grace is present and active in his image.

HENRI J. M. NOUWEN
BEHOLD THE BEAUTY OF THE LORD

In contrast to the more familiar art of the West, icons are made according to age-old rules. Their forms and colors depend not merely upon the imagination and taste of the iconographer, but are handed down from generation to generation in obedience to venerable traditions. The iconographer's first concern is not to make himself known but to proclaim God's kingdom through his art. Icons are meant to have a place in the sacred liturgy and are thus painted in accordance with the demands of the liturgy. As does the liturgy itself, icons try to give us a glimpse of heaven.

This explains why icons are not easy to "see." They do not immediately speak to our senses. . . . They do not reveal themselves to us at first sight. It is only gradually, after a patient, prayerful presence that they start speaking to us. And as they speak, they speak more to our inner than to our outer senses. They speak to the heart that searches for God.

THE ICON OF THE VIRGIN OF VLADIMIR

Because I have used the icon of the Virgin of Vladimir for the cover art of this book, it seems appropriate to include Nouwen's meditation on this special image.

The icon of the Virgin of Vladimir has gradually become for me a strong yet gentle invitation to leave the compulsive and divisive milieu of the world, and to enter the liberating and uniting milieu of God. Over the years I had seen the icon in so many homes, rectories and convents that I hardly paid any attention to it. . . . But when during a long, silent retreat a large reproduction of the Virgin of Vladimir was placed on my table, I gradually began to discover the inner nature of the icon. As I prayed daily to the Virgin, I felt drawn into its mysterious intimacy and came to "know by heart" its urgent invitation to belong to God. . . .

Contemplating this icon was a profound experience for me. It was the experience of being lifted up through the intercession of the Blessed Mother into the inner life of God.

—*Behold the Beauty of the Lord*

ICONS AND SACRED ART TODAY

The Church today encourages expression of the divine in icons and sacred art. The *Constitution on the Sacred Liturgy* describes the importance of religious art, especially as it is used to offer praise and glory to God:

> The fine arts are rightly classed among the noblest activities of man's genius; this is especially true of religious art and of its highest manifestation, sacred art. Of their nature the arts are directed toward expressing in some way the infinite beauty of God in works made by human hands. Their dedication to the increase of God's praise and of his glory is more complete, the more exclusively they are devoted to turning men's minds devoutly toward God.
>
> For that reason holy Mother Church has always been the patron of the fine arts and has ever sought their noble ministry, to the end especially that all things set apart for use in divine worship should be worthy, becoming, and beautiful, signs and symbols of things supernatural. (*Constitution on the Sacred Liturgy*, no. 122)

WORKS CITED

The following is a list of the books and articles from which I have quoted in the preceding chapters.

Cunningham, Lawrence S. *The Meaning of Saints*. San Francisco: Harper and Row, 1980.

Delany, H. P. *The Miraculous Medal*. Dublin: Clonmore and Reynolds, 1954.

Egan, Harvey. "'The Devout Christian of the Future Will . . . Be a Mystic.' Mysticism and Karl Rahner's Theology," *Theology and Discovery: Essays in Honor of Karl Rahner, S.J.* Milwaukee: Marquette University, 1980.

Eliot, T. S. *Four Quartets*. New York: Harcourt Brace Jovanovich, 1943.

Flannery, Austin, O.P., ed. *Vatican Council II: The Conciliar and Post Conciliar Documents*. Vatican Collection, Vol. 1. Northport, New York: Costello Publishing Company, 1992.

Liguori, St. Alphonsus. *Novena to the Sacred Heart of Jesus*. Liguori, Missouri: Liguori, 1997.

McBrien, Richard P., ed. *The HarperCollins Encyclopedia of Catholicism*. San Francisco: HarperCollins, 1995.

New Catholic Encyclopedia, Vol. 1 - Vol. 15. Washington, D.C.: Catholic University of America Press, 1967-79.

Norris, Kathleen. *The Cloister Walk*. New York: Riverhead Books, 1996.

Nouwen, Henri J. M. *Behold the Beauty of the Lord*. Notre Dame, Indiana: Ave Maria Press, 1987.

Quoist, Michel. *Prayers*. Kansas City: Sheed & Ward, 1963.

Rahner, Karl. *Prayers for a Lifetime*. New York: Crossroad, 1995.

The Rule of St. Benedict in English. Collegeville, Minnesota: Liturgical Press, 1981.

The Scapular of Our Lady of Mount Carmel. Middletown, New York: National Shrine of Our Lady of Mount Carmel, 1995.

Schillebeeckx, Edward. *Mary, Mother of the Redemption*. Kansas City, Missouri: Sheed and Ward, 1964.

Study Text VII: The Liturgy of the Hours. Washington, D.C.: United States Catholic Conference, 1981.

Thurston, Herbert. *The Stations of the Cross*. New York: Benziger, 1906.

Von Balthasar, Hans Urs. *The von Balthasar Reader*. New York: Crossroad, 1997.

Walsh, Michael. *Dictionary of Catholic Devotions*. San Francisco: HarperCollins, 1993.

Woodward, Kenneth L. *Making Saints*. New York: Simon and Schuster, 1990.

ACKNOWLEDGMENTS

We wish to acknowledge the following publishers for permission to reprint previously published material.

Excerpted from *Behold the Beauty of the Lord* by Henri J. M. Nouwen. Copyright © 1987 by Ave Maria Press, Notre Dame, IN 46556. Used with permission of the publisher.

From *The Cloister Walk*. Reprinted by permission of Riverhead Books, a division of The Putnam Publishing Group from THE CLOISTER WALK by Kathleen Norris. Copyright © 1996 by Kathleen Norris. Other rights, reprinted by permission of Janklow & Nesbit.

Excerpts as submitted from THE HARPERCOLLINS ENCYCLOPEDIA OF CATHOLICISM by Richard P. McBrien. Copyright © 1995 by HarperCollins Publishers, Inc. Reprinted by permission of HarperCollins Publishers, Inc.

Excerpt from "Little Gidding" in FOUR QUARTETS, copyright © 1943 by T. S. Eliot and renewed 1971 by Esme Valerie Eliot, reprinted by permission of Harcourt Brace & Company. English language rights, reprinted by permission of Faber and Faber Ltd.

From *Making Saints*. Reprinted with the permission of Simon & Schuster from MAKING SAINTS by Kenneth L. Woodward. Copyright © 1990 by Kenneth Woodward. English language rights in the United Kingdom and its territories, reprinted by permission of International Creative Management, Inc.

From *Mary, Mother of the Redemption* by Edward Schillebeeckx, O.P. Copyright © 1964 by Sheed & Ward. Reprinted with the permission of Sheed & Ward, 115 E. Armour Blvd., Kansas City, MO 64111.

From *New Catholic Encyclopedia* Vol. 1 - Vol. 15. Copyright © 1967-1979 by The Catholic University of America Press. Reprinted by permission of The Catholic University of America Press.

From *Novena to the Sacred Heart of Jesus* by St. Alphonsus Liguori. Copyright © 1997 by Liguori Publications. Reprinted by permission of Liguori Publications.

From *Prayers* by Michel Quoist. Copyright © 1963 by Sheed &

Ward. Reprinted with the permission of Sheed & Ward, 115 E. Armour Blvd., Kansas City, MO 64111.

From *Prayers for Meditation*, with Hugo Rahner. Translated by Rosaleen Brennan. New York: Herder and Herder, 1962. © 1962 by Herder KG. Originally published as *Gebete der Einkehr* (1958). Reprinted along with *Worte ins Schweigen* under the title *Worte ins Schweigen, Gebete der Einkehr*. Freiburg: Verlag Herder, 1973. Reprinted by permission of T&T Clark Ltd. and Verlag Herder.

From *The Scapular of Our Lady of Mount Carmel*. Copyright © 1995 by National Shrine of Our Lady of Mount Carmel. Reprinted by permission of National Shrine of Our Lady of Mount Carmel.

Excerpts from *Study Text 7: The Liturgy of the Hours*. Copyright © 1981 United States Catholic Conference, Inc., Washington, DC. Used with permission. All Rights Reserved.

From *Theological Investigations* by Karl Rahner, published and copyright © 1966 by Darton, Longman & Todd Ltd. and used by permission of the publishers. Originally published as the first part of *Schriften zur Theologie VII*. Einsiedeln: Benziger Verlag, 1966. Reprinted by permission of Benziger Verlag AG Zürich.

From *Watch and Pray with Me*. Translated by William V. Dych, S.J. New York: Herder and Herder, 1966. Originally published as *Heilige Stunde und Passionsandacht* (1949). Freiburg: Verlag Herder, 1965. Reprinted by permission of T&T Clark Ltd. and Verlag Herder.

Excerpts from *Vatican Council II: The Conciliar and Post Conciliar Documents*, *New Revised Edition* edited by Austin Flannery, O.P., copyright © 1992, Costello Publishing Company, Inc., Northport, NY are used by permission of the publisher, all rights reserved. No part of these excerpts may be reproduced, stored in a retrieval system, or transmitted in any form or by any means—electronic, mechanical, photocopying, recording or otherwise, without express permission of Costello Publishing Company.

From *The von Balthasar Reader* by Hans Urs von Balthasar. English translation copyright © 1982 by The Crossroad Publishing Company. Reprinted by permission of The Crossroad Publishing Company. Originally published as *Aus der Fülle des Glaubens—Ein Lesebuch*. Copyright © by Johannes Verlag. Reprinted by permission of Archiv Hans Urs von Balthasar and T&T Clark Ltd.